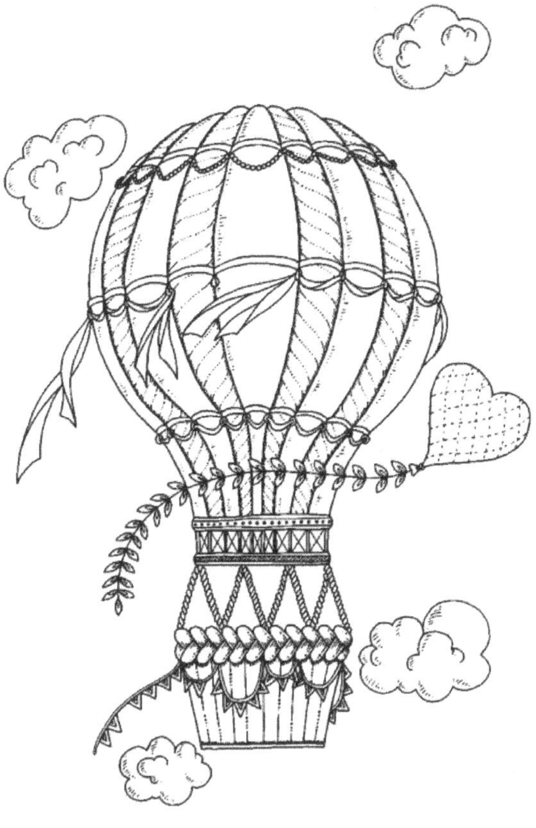

BALLOON PUBLISHING

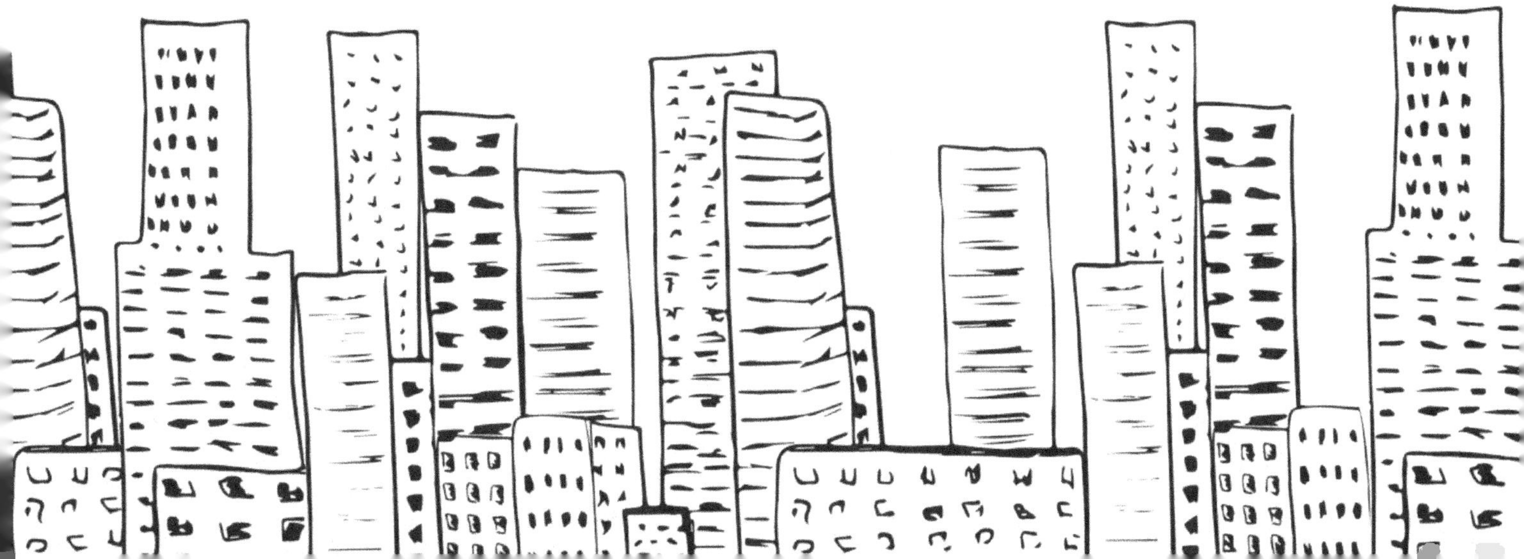

COLOR TEST PAGE

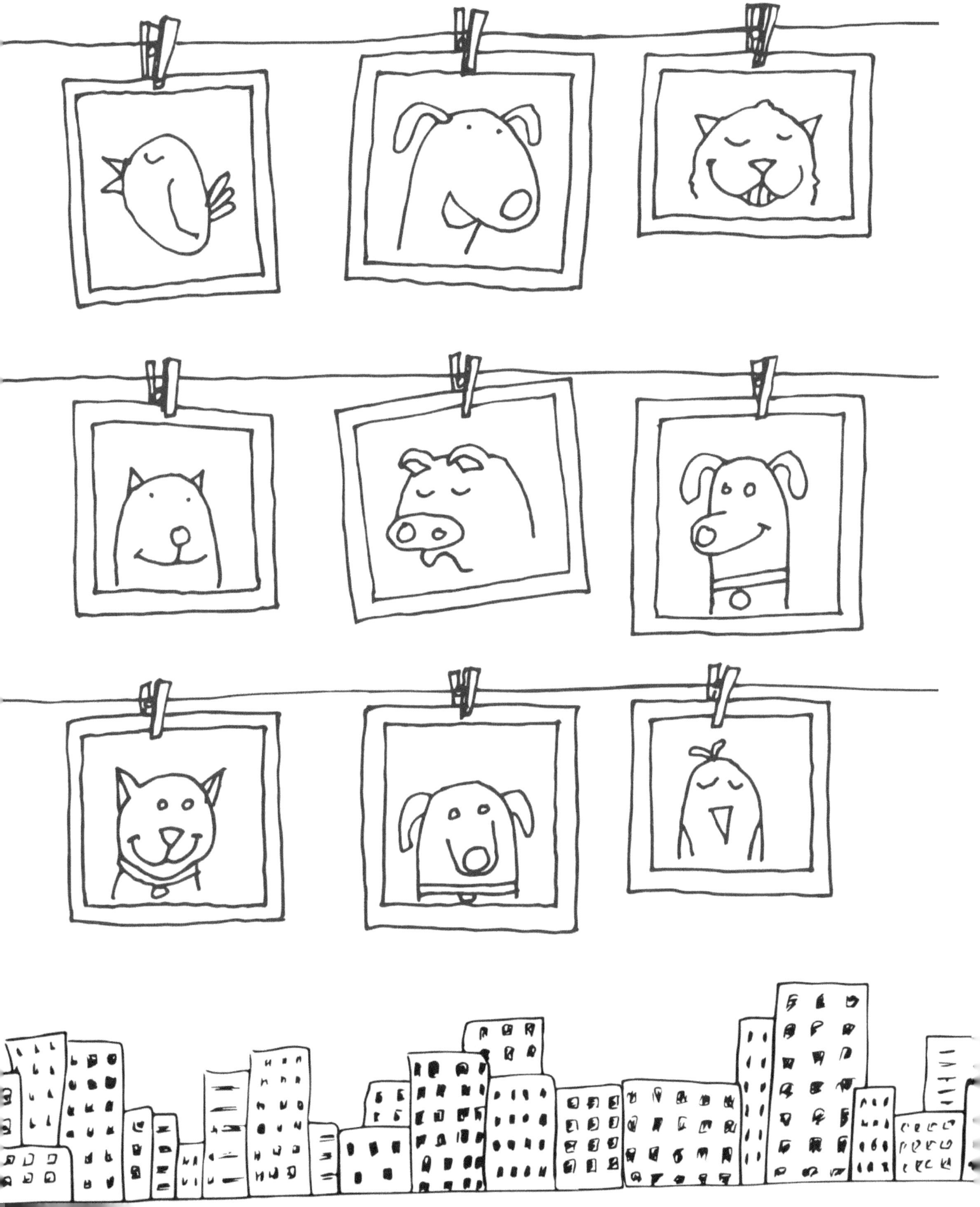

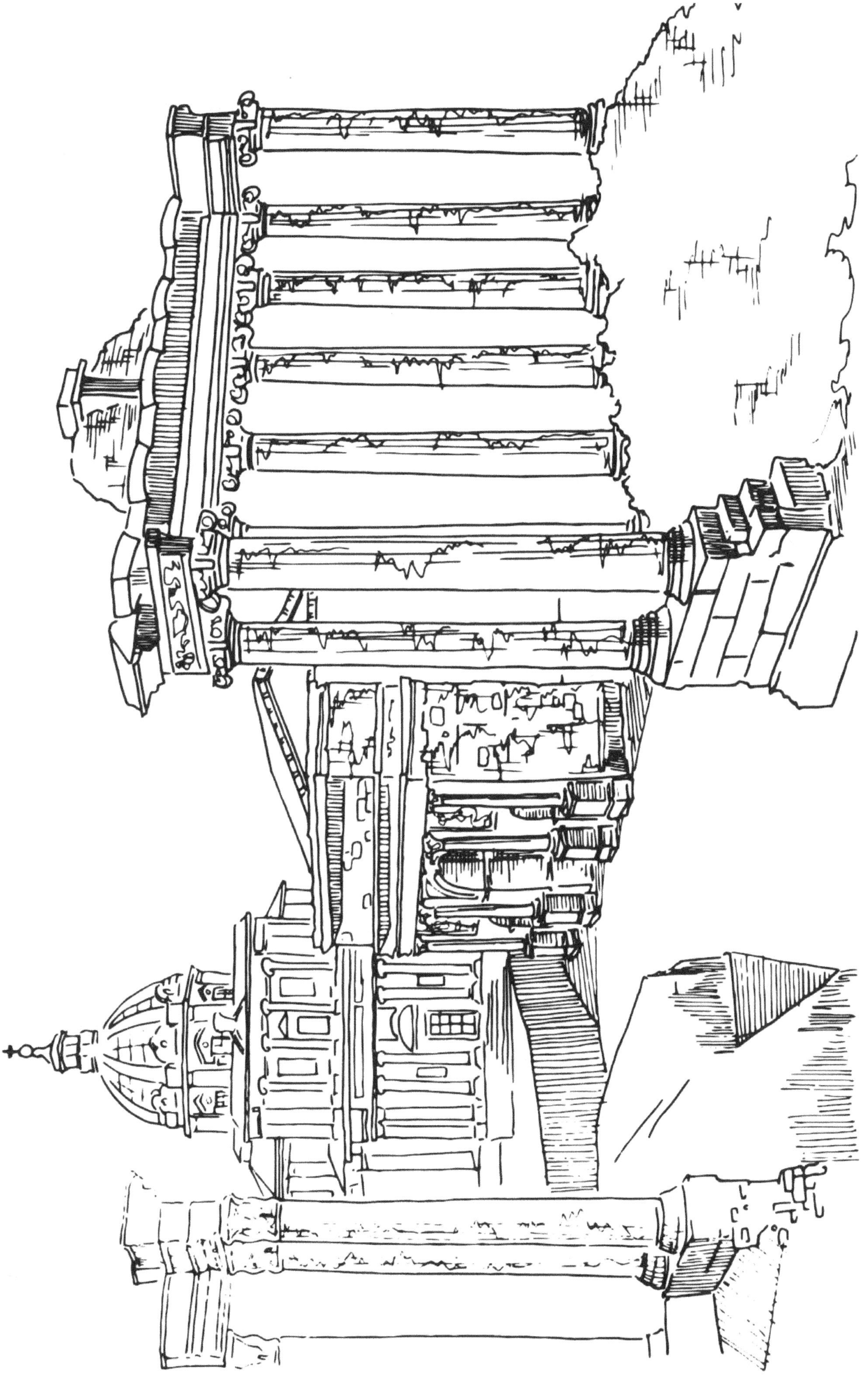

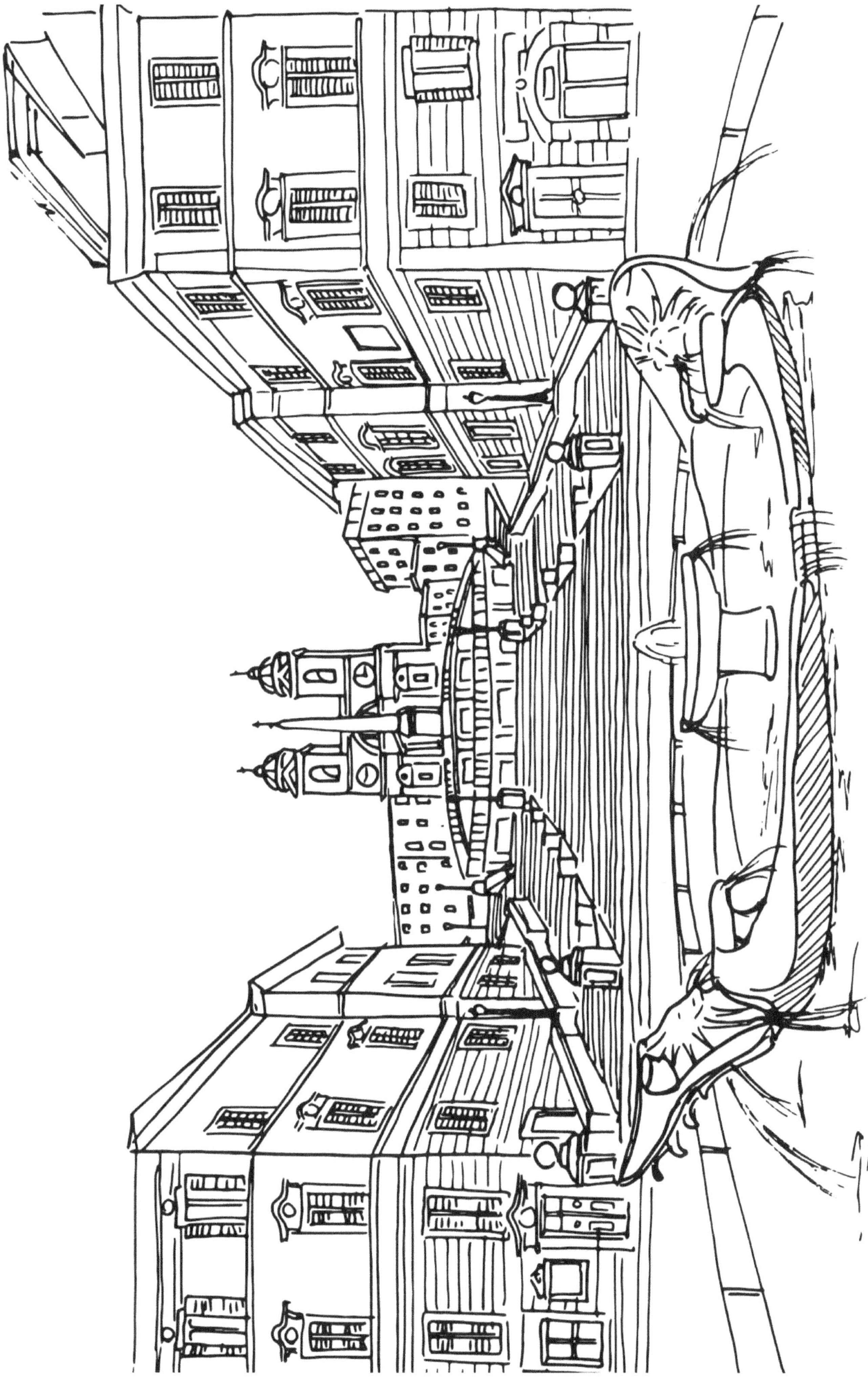

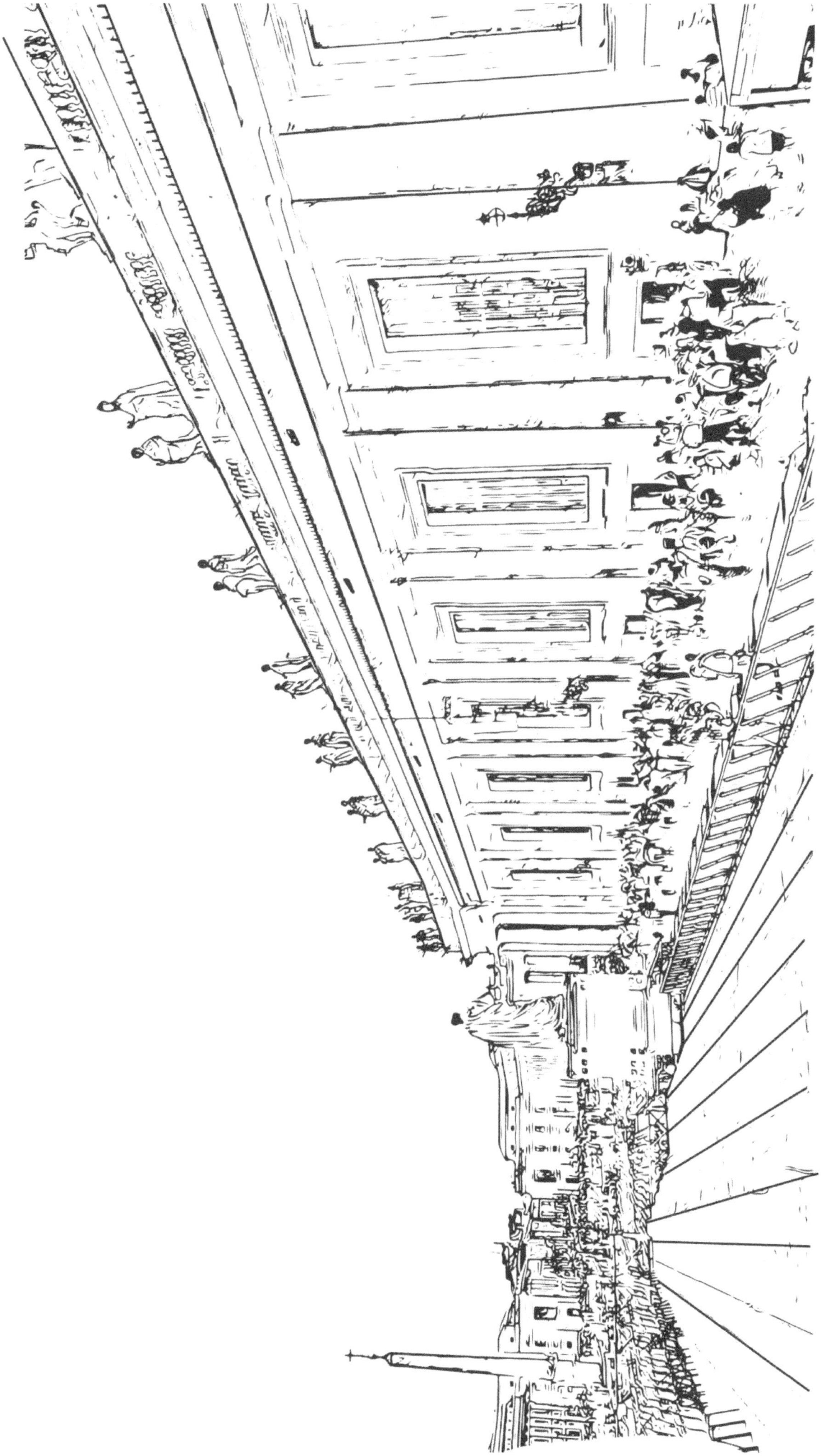

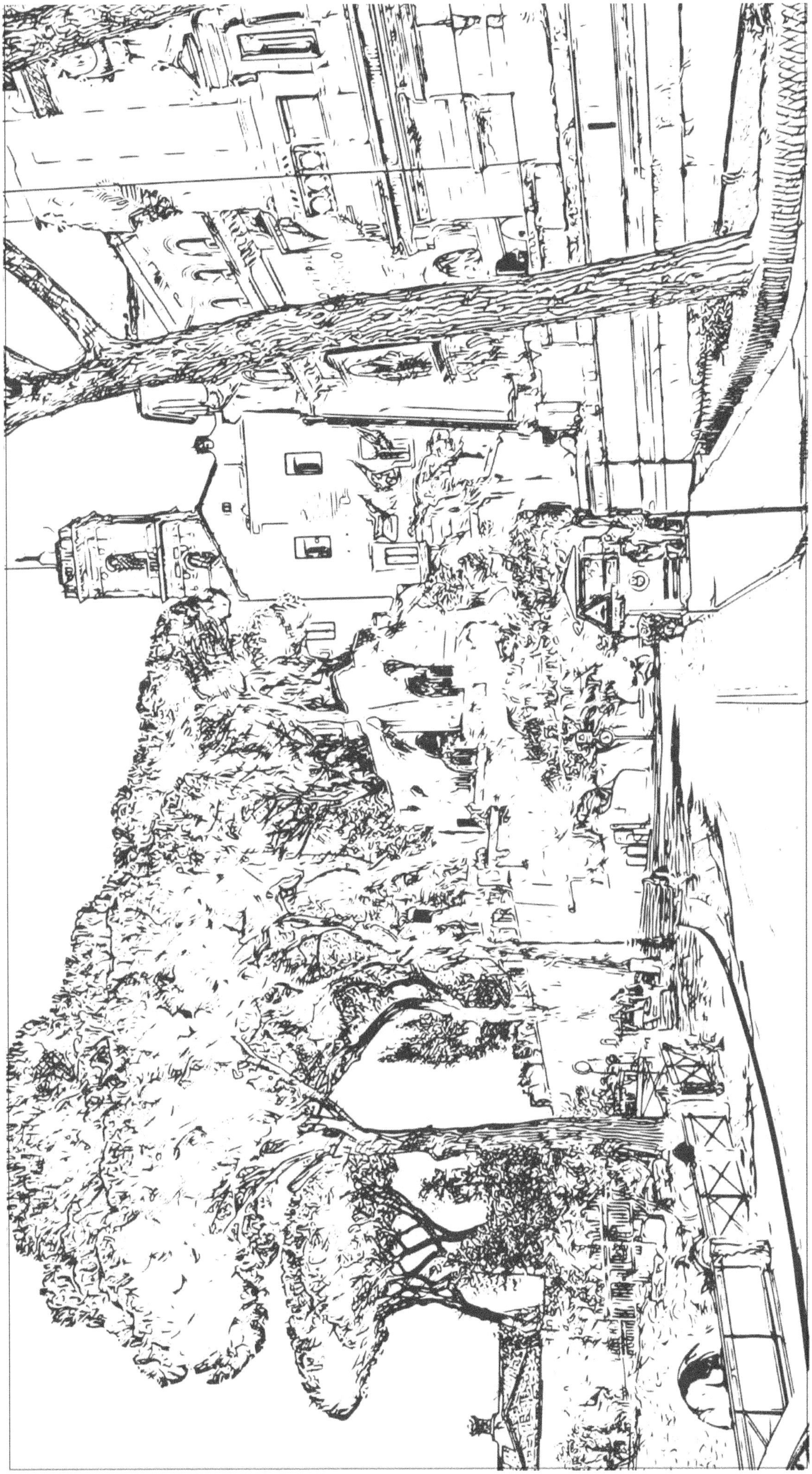

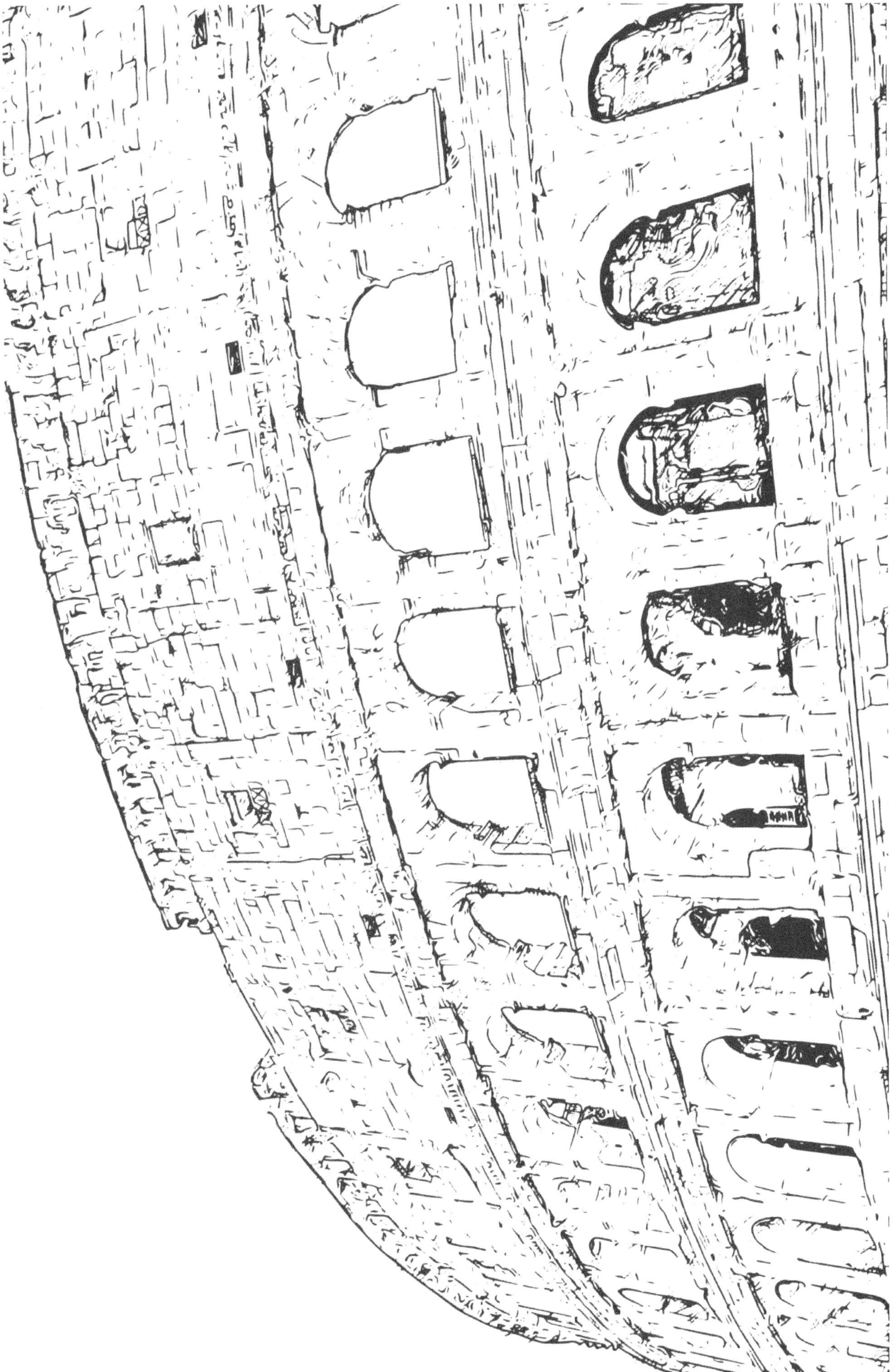

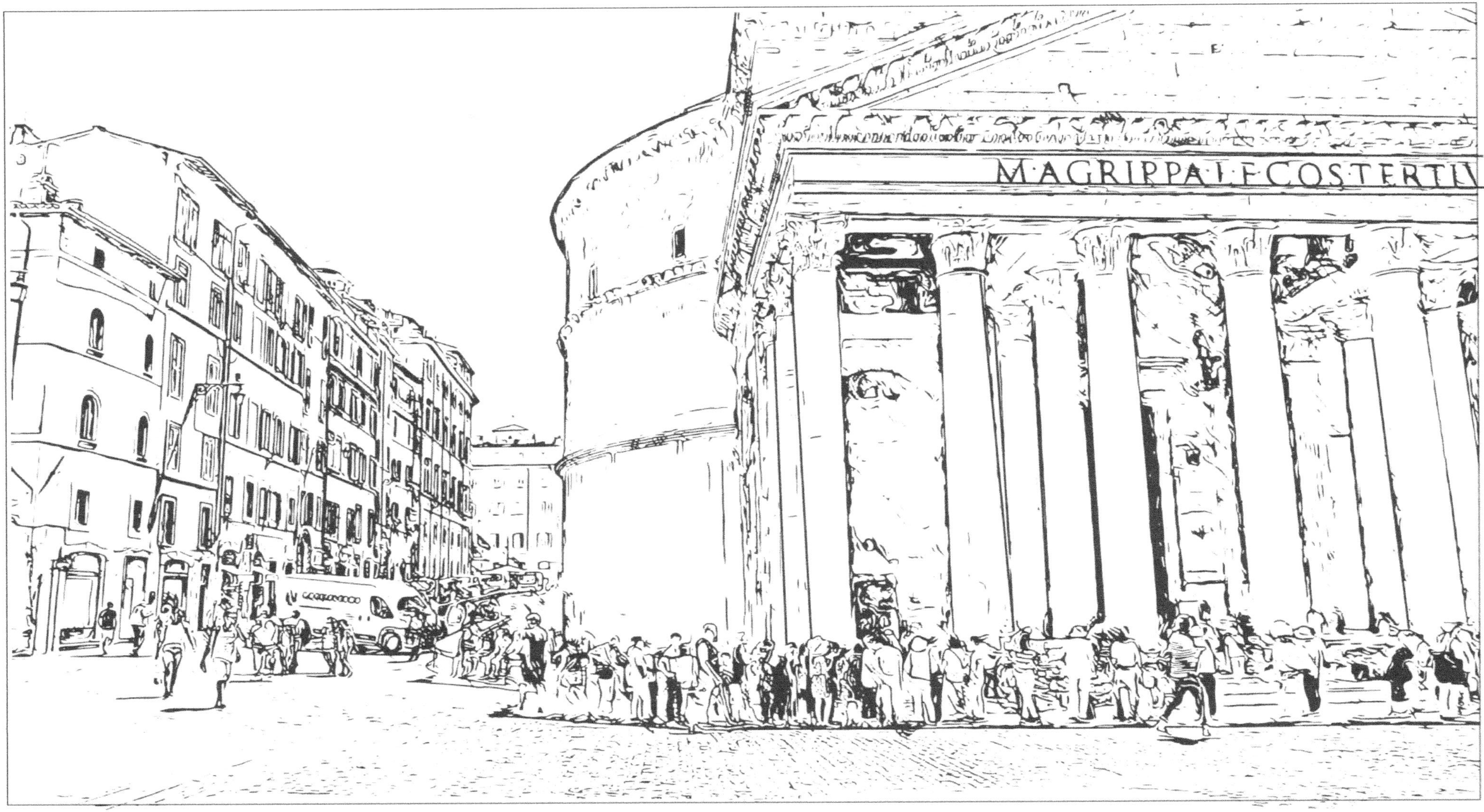
M·AGRIPPA·L·F·COS·TERTIV

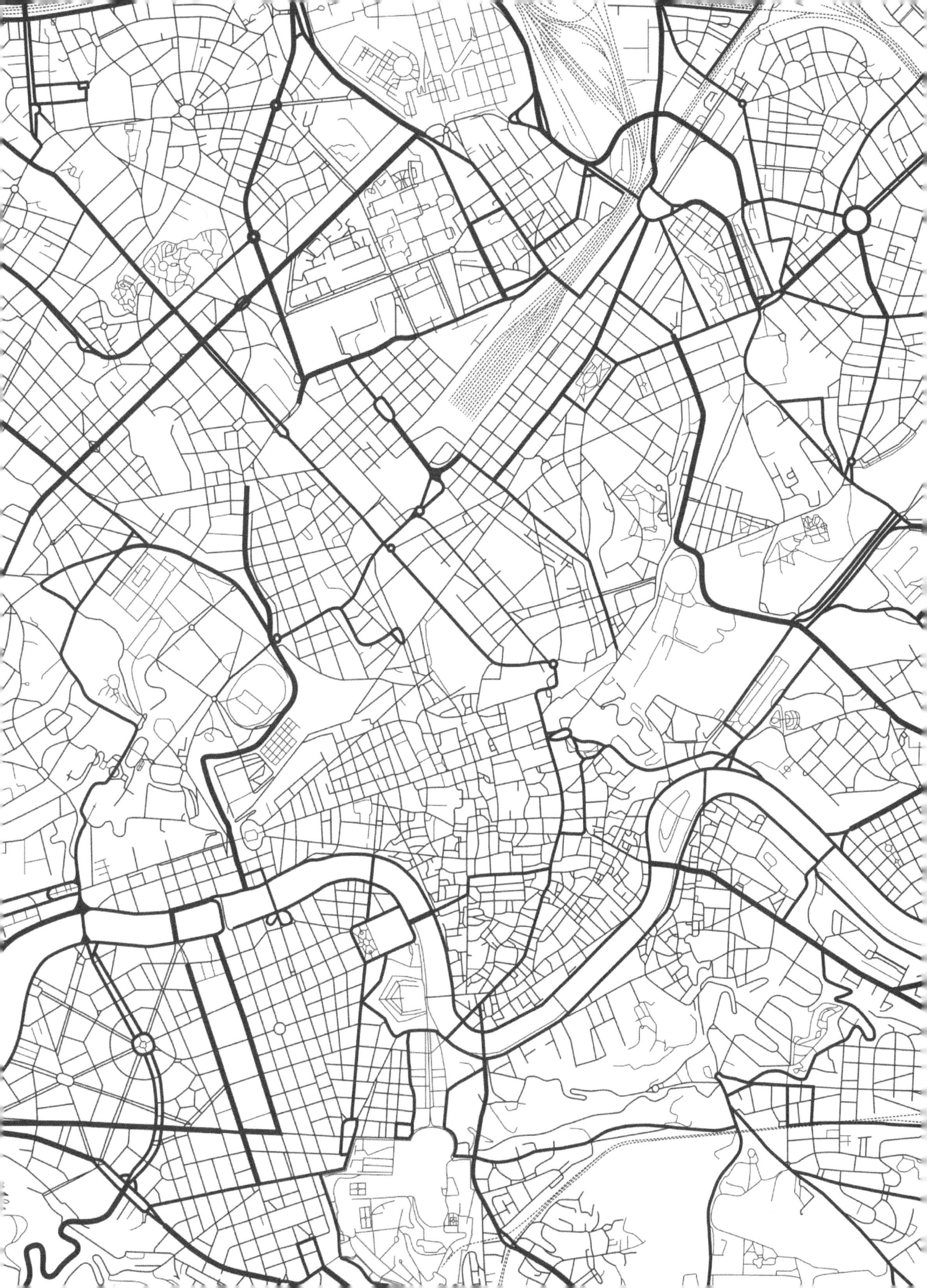

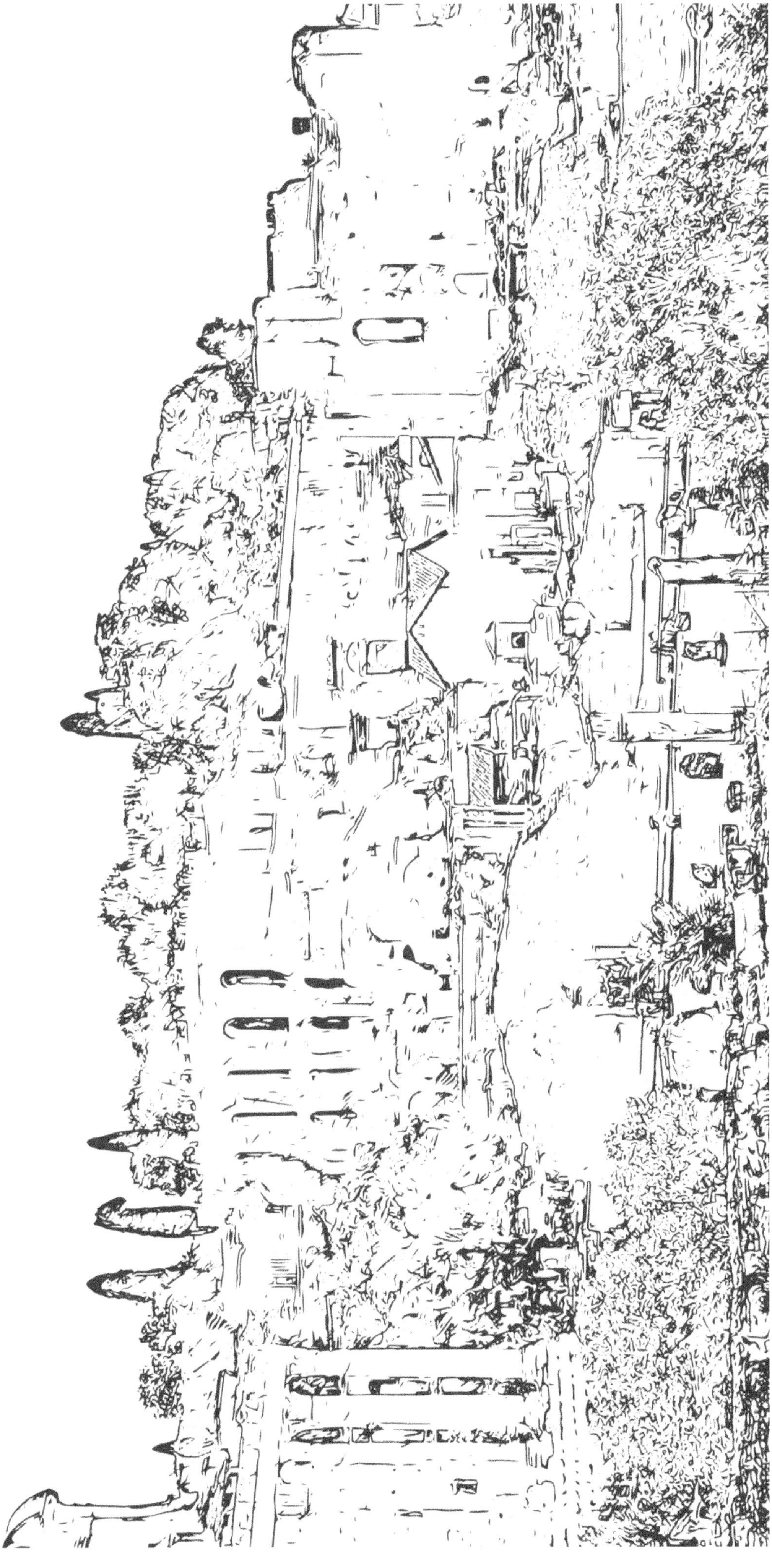

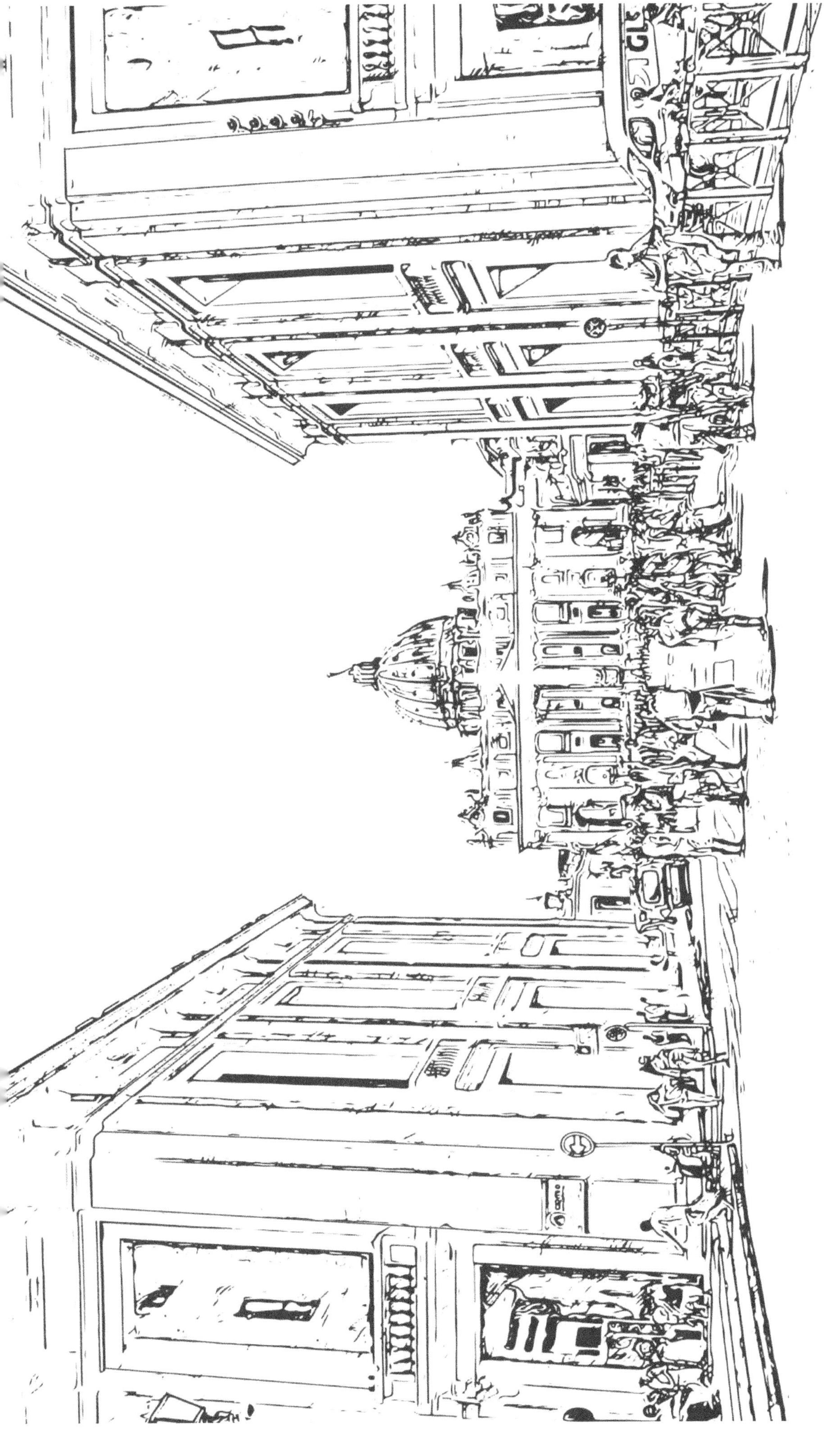

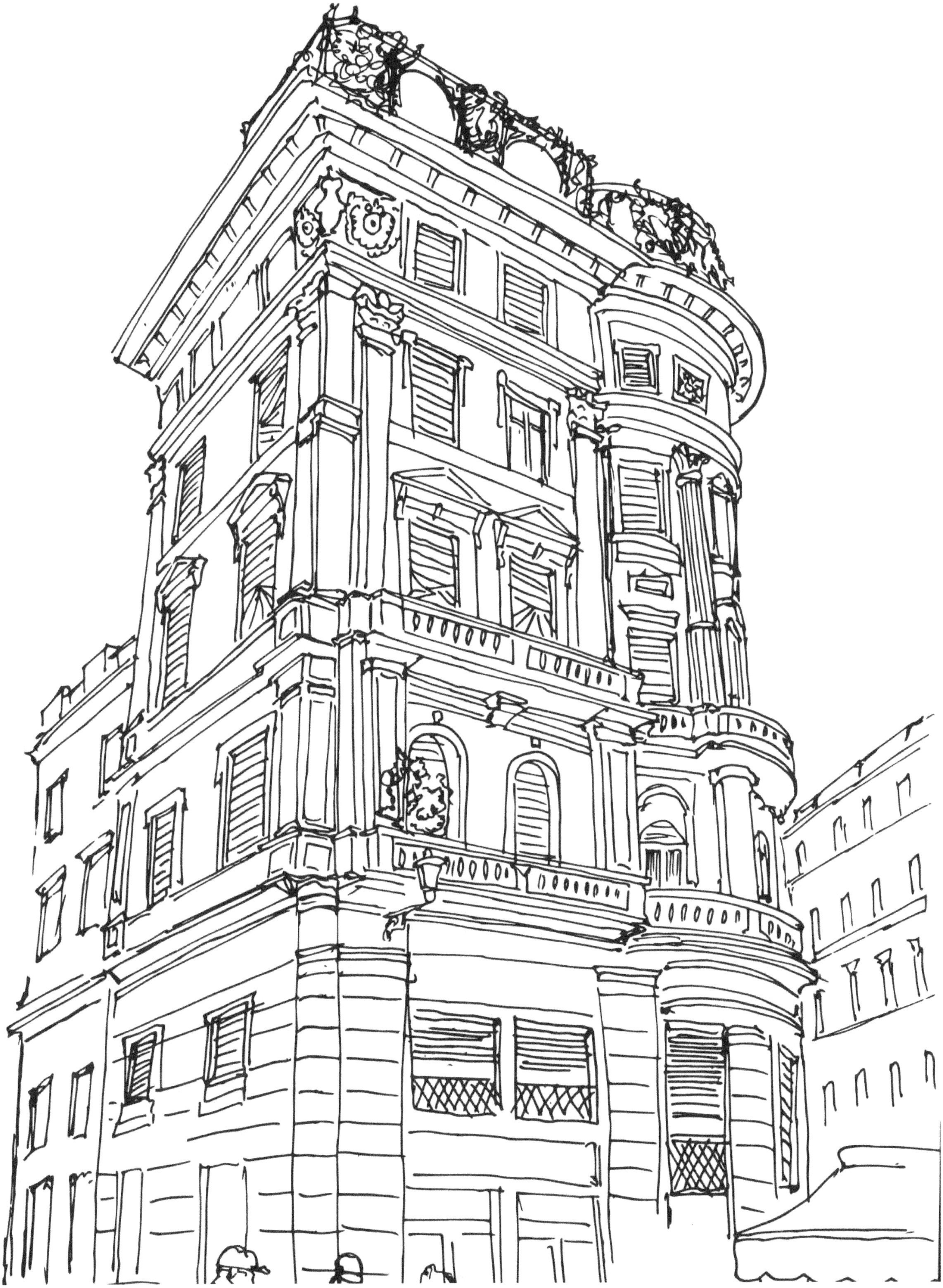

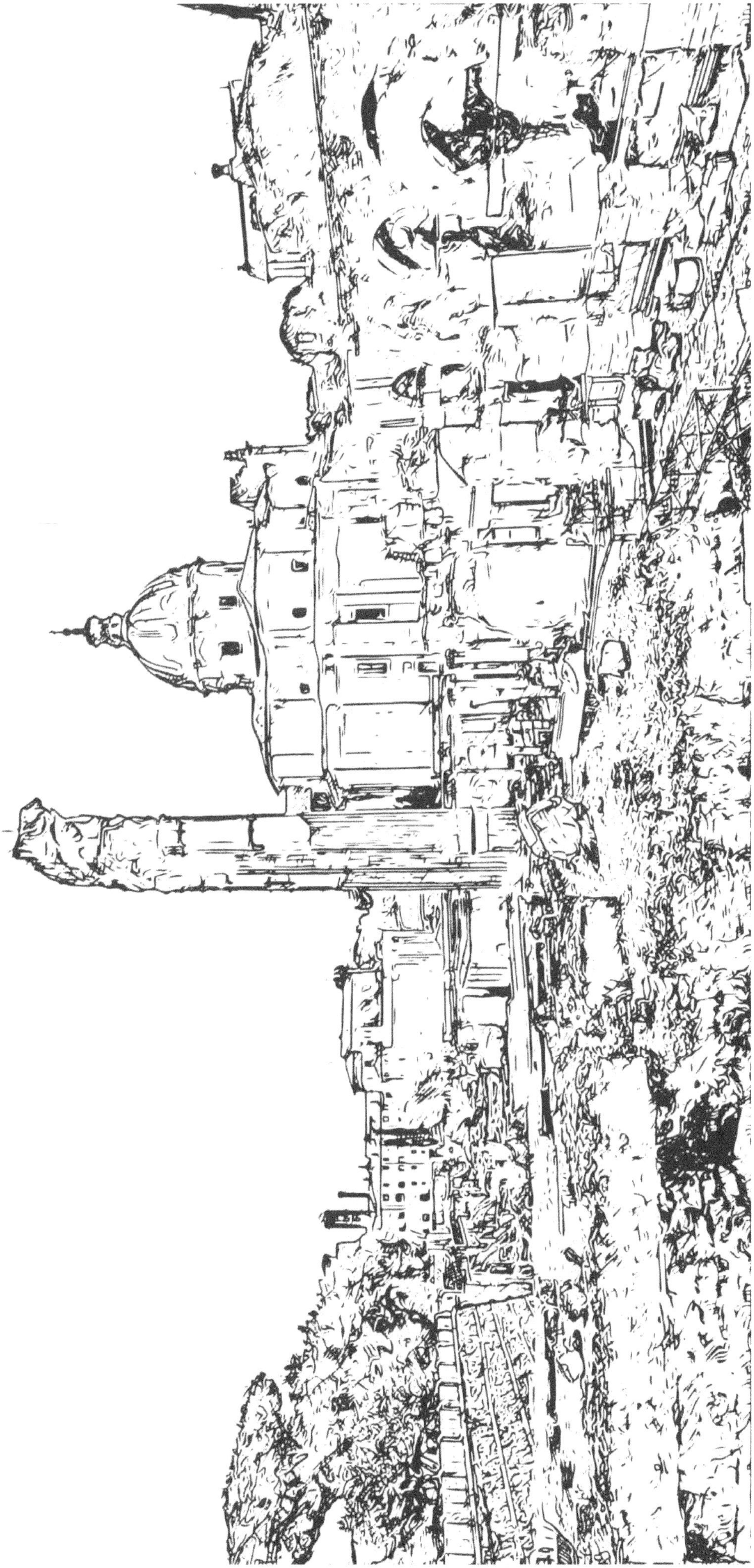

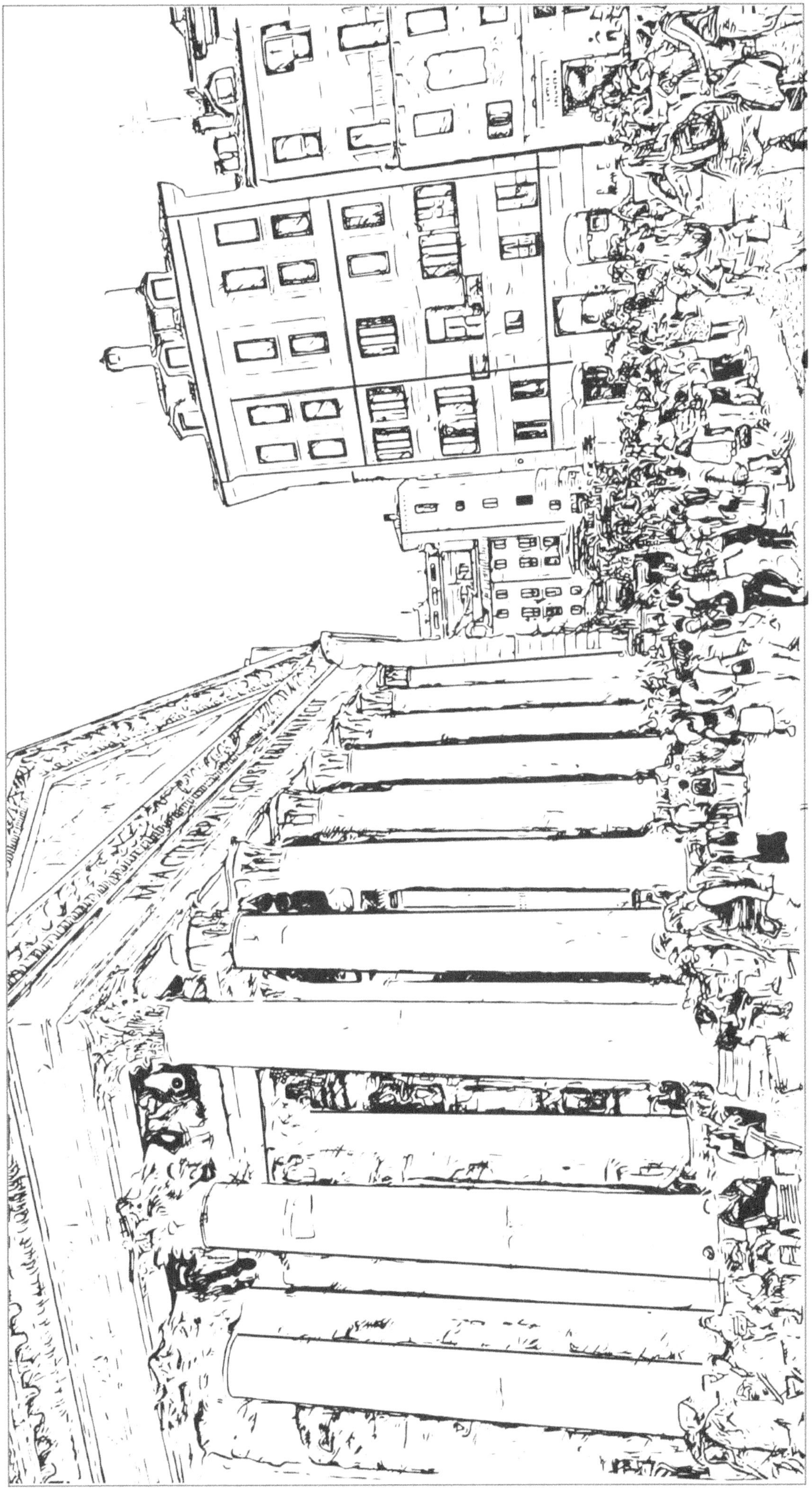

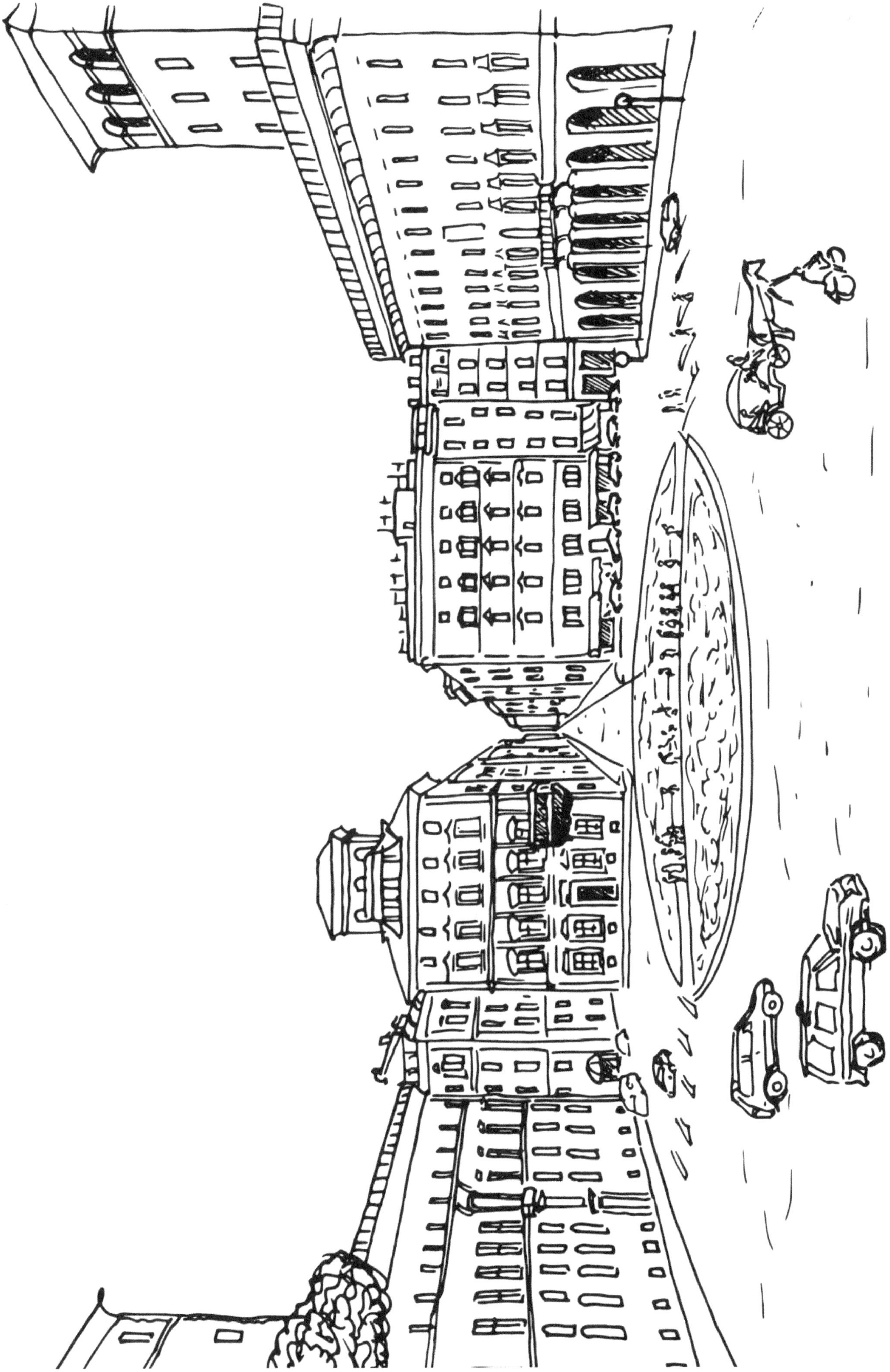

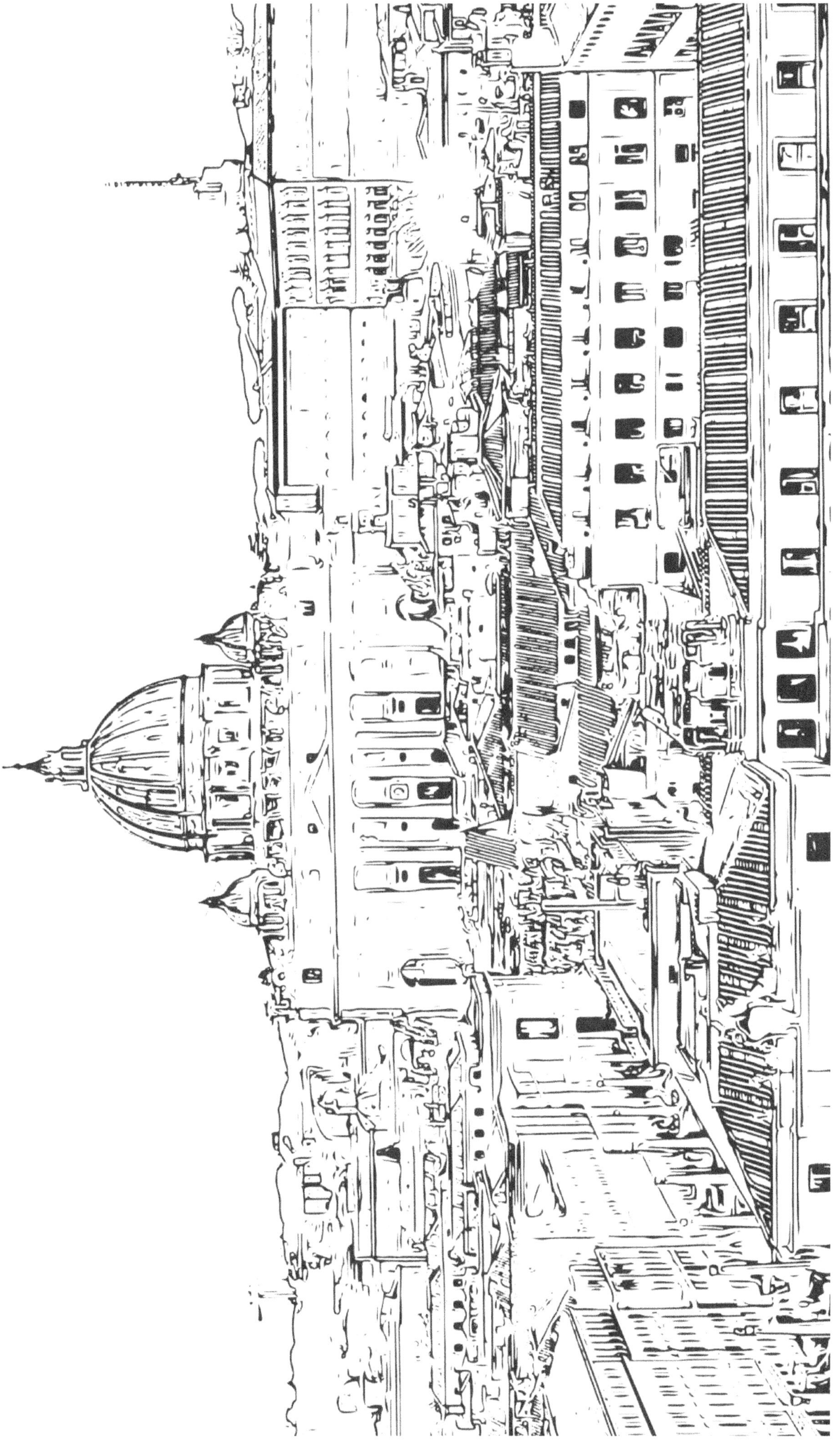

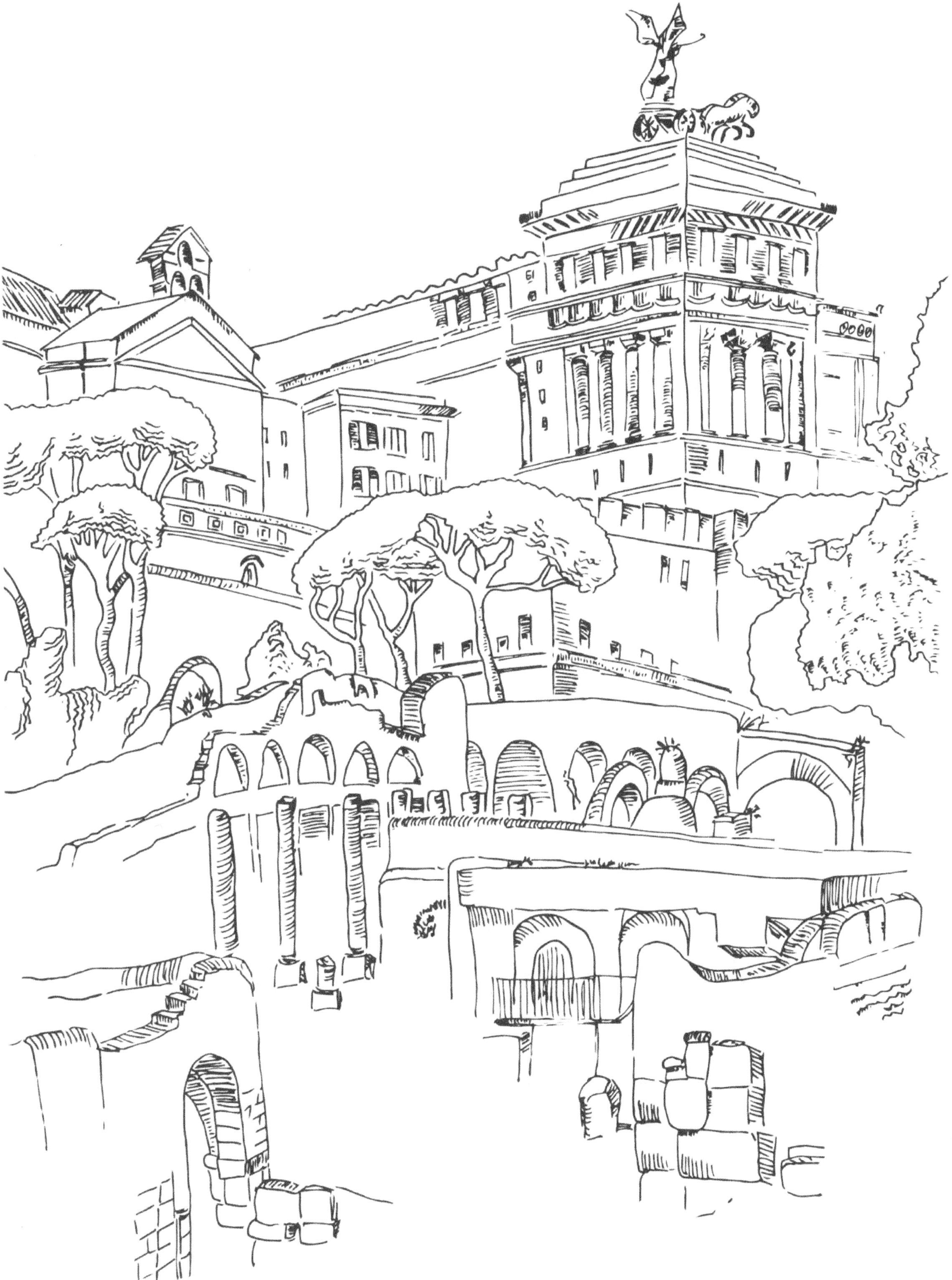

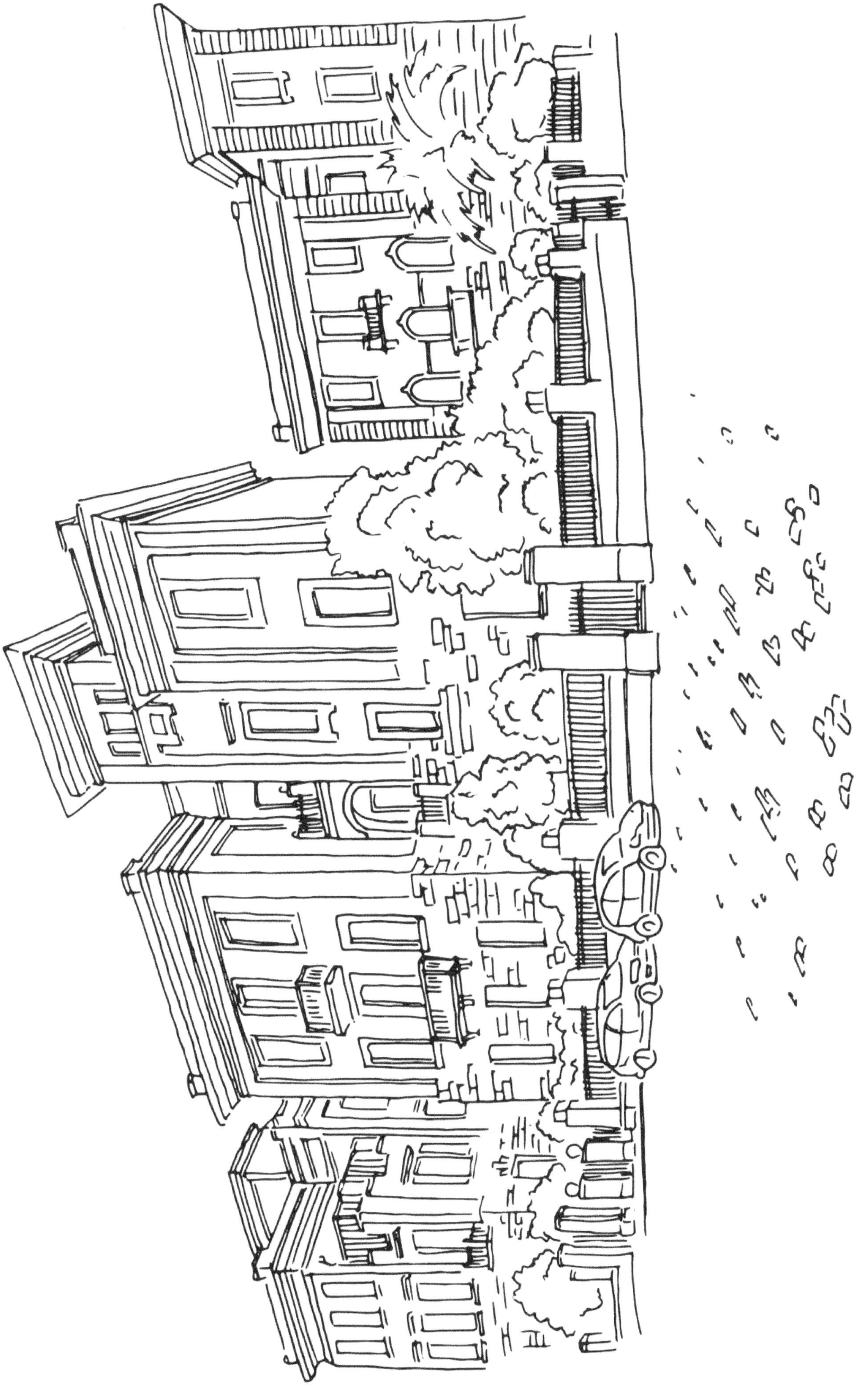

ROME

ITALY

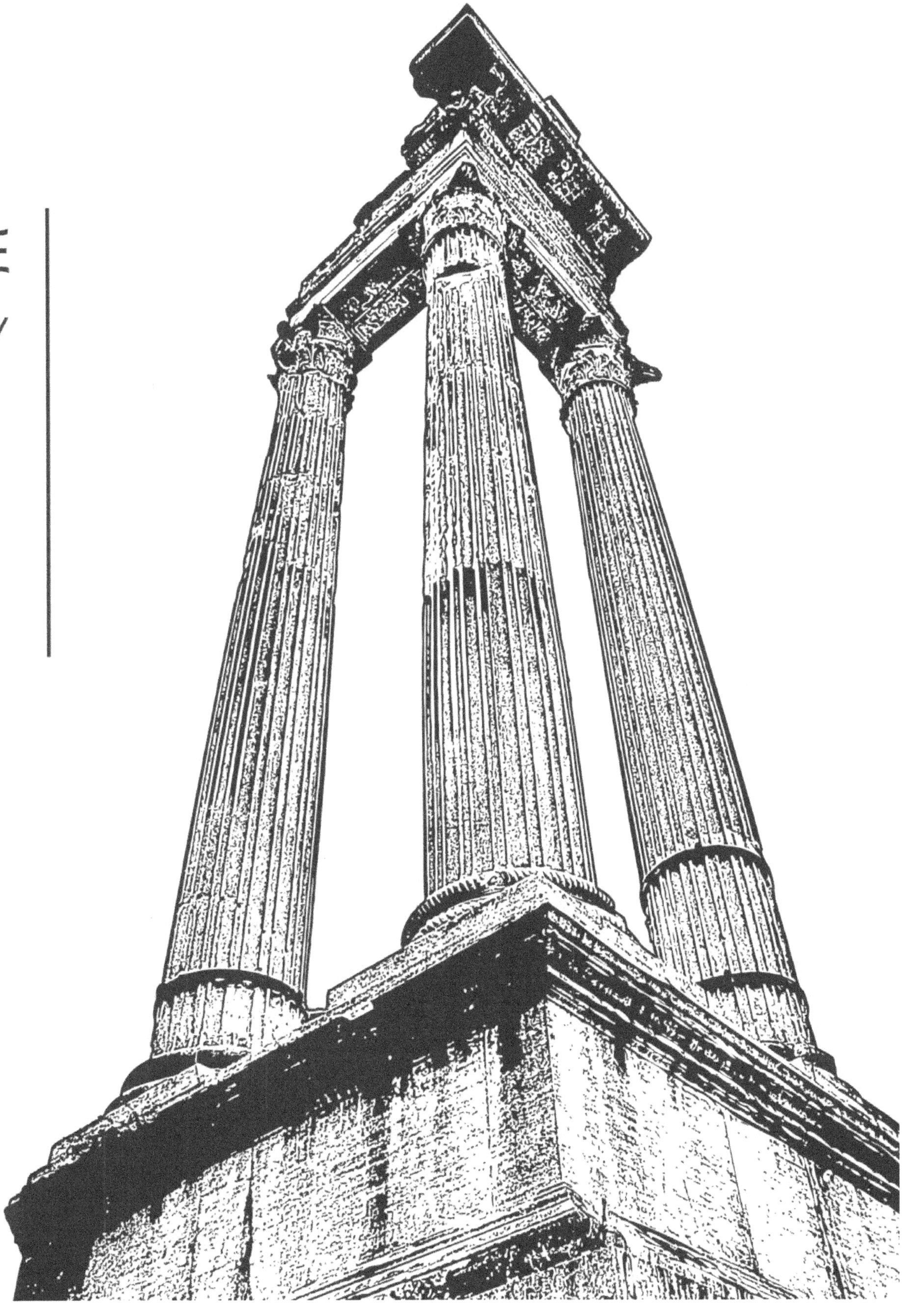

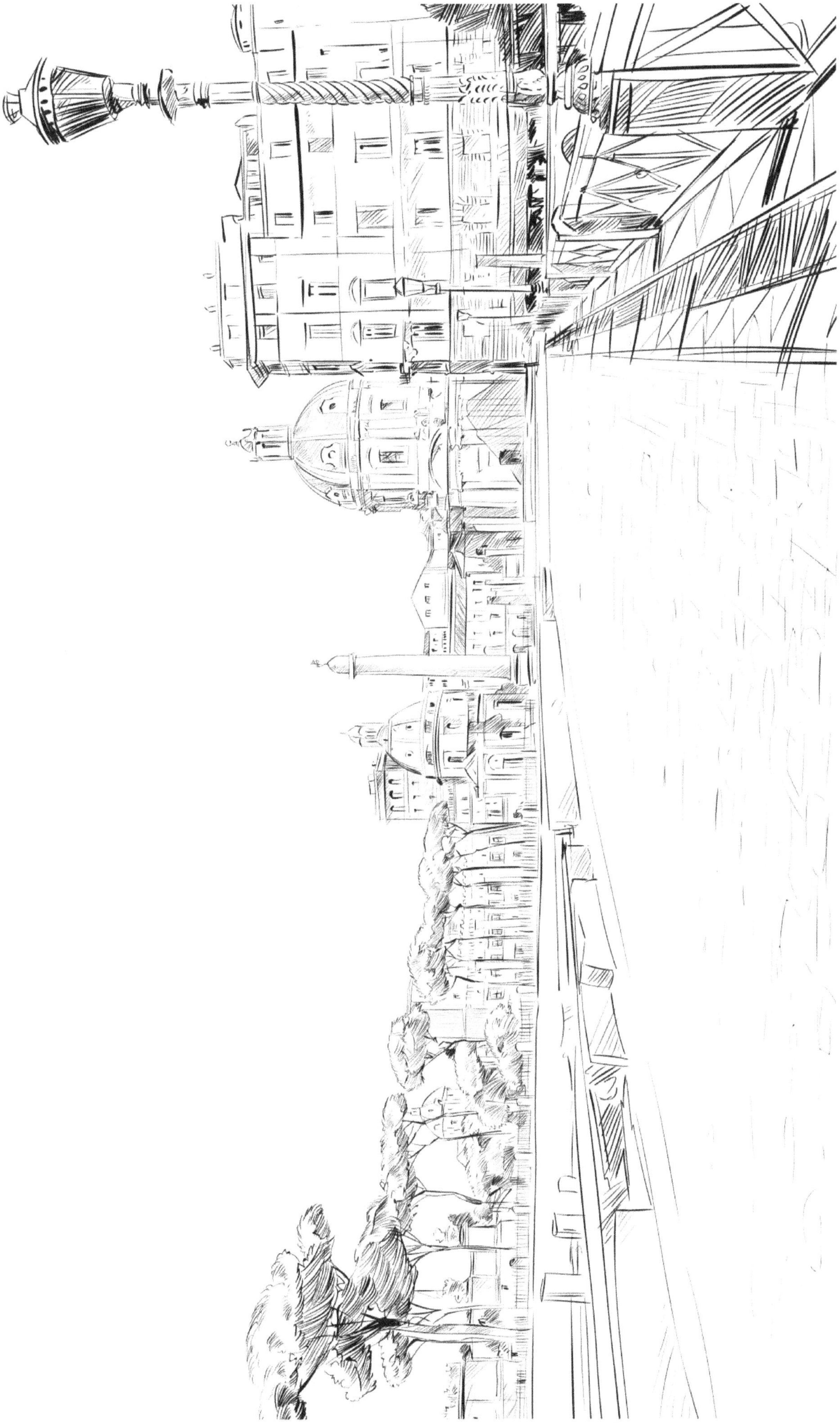

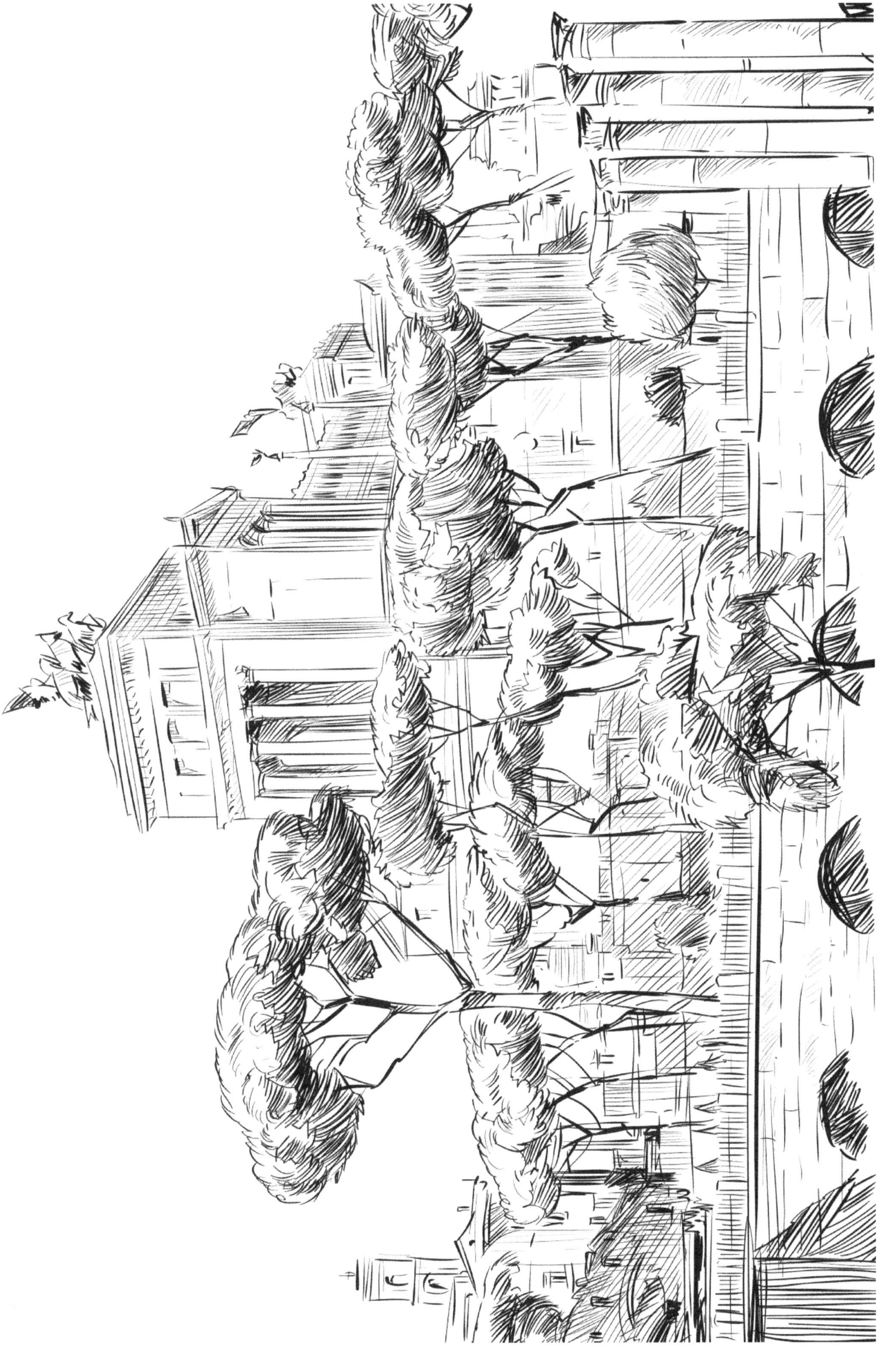

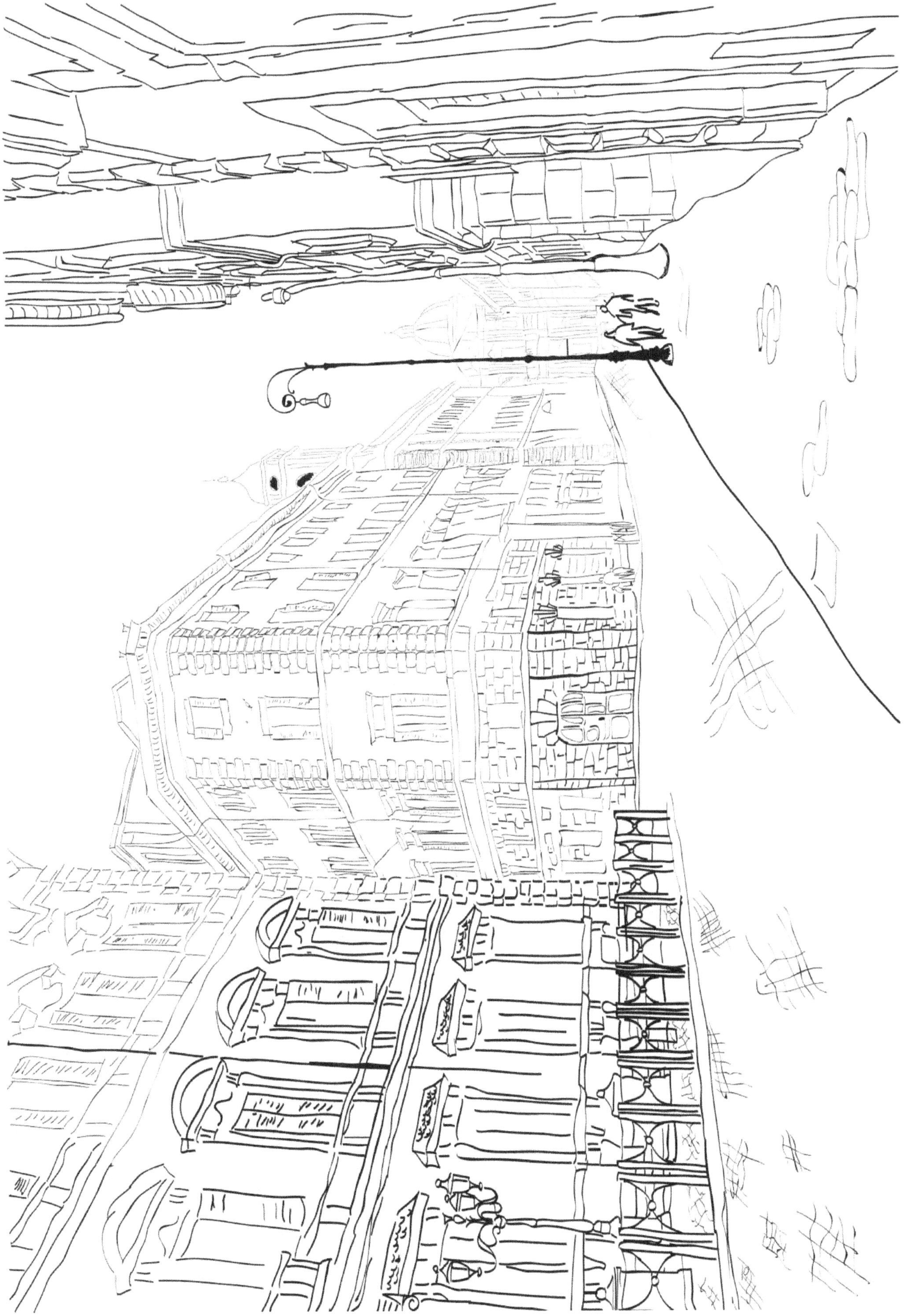

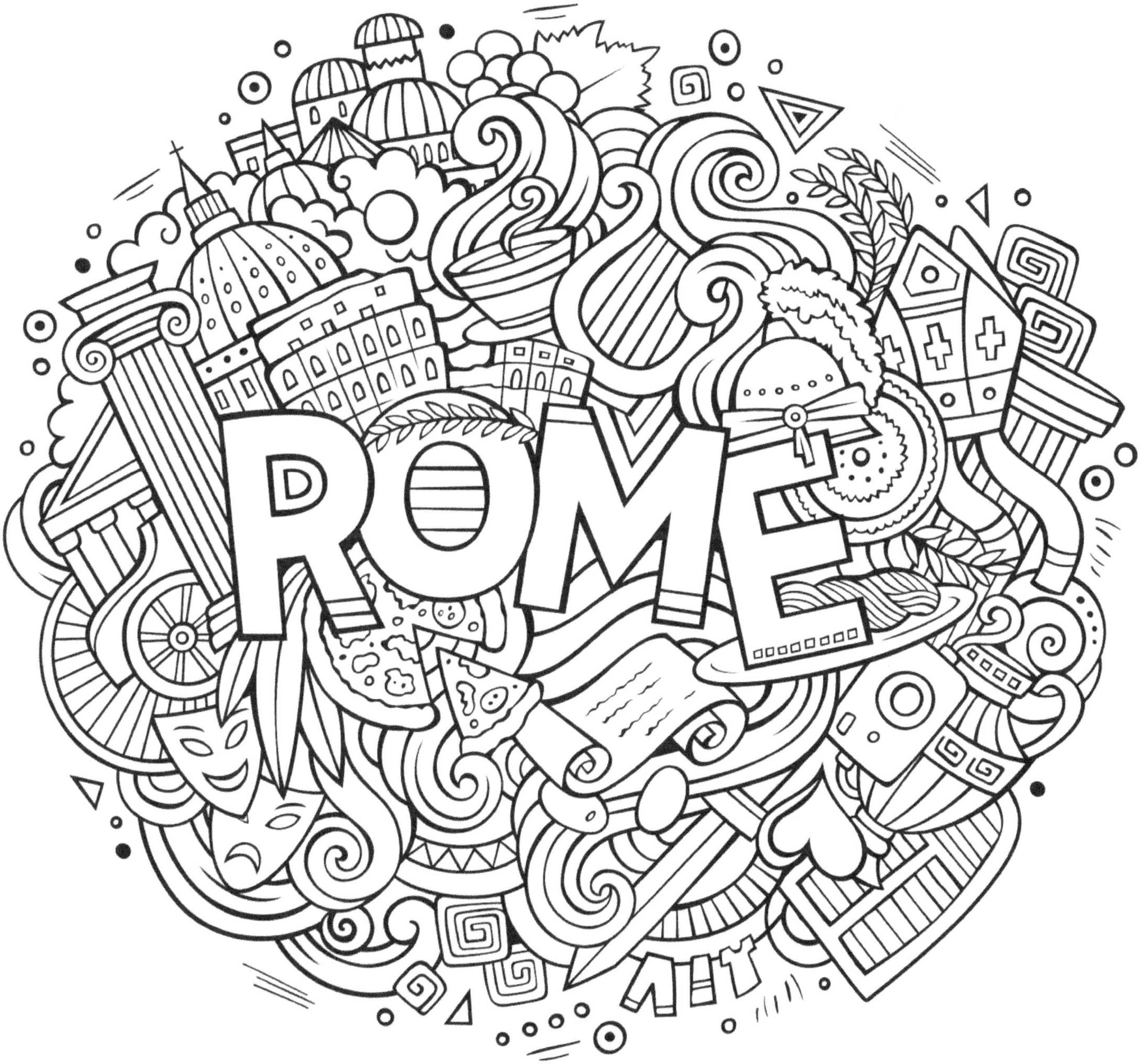
ROME

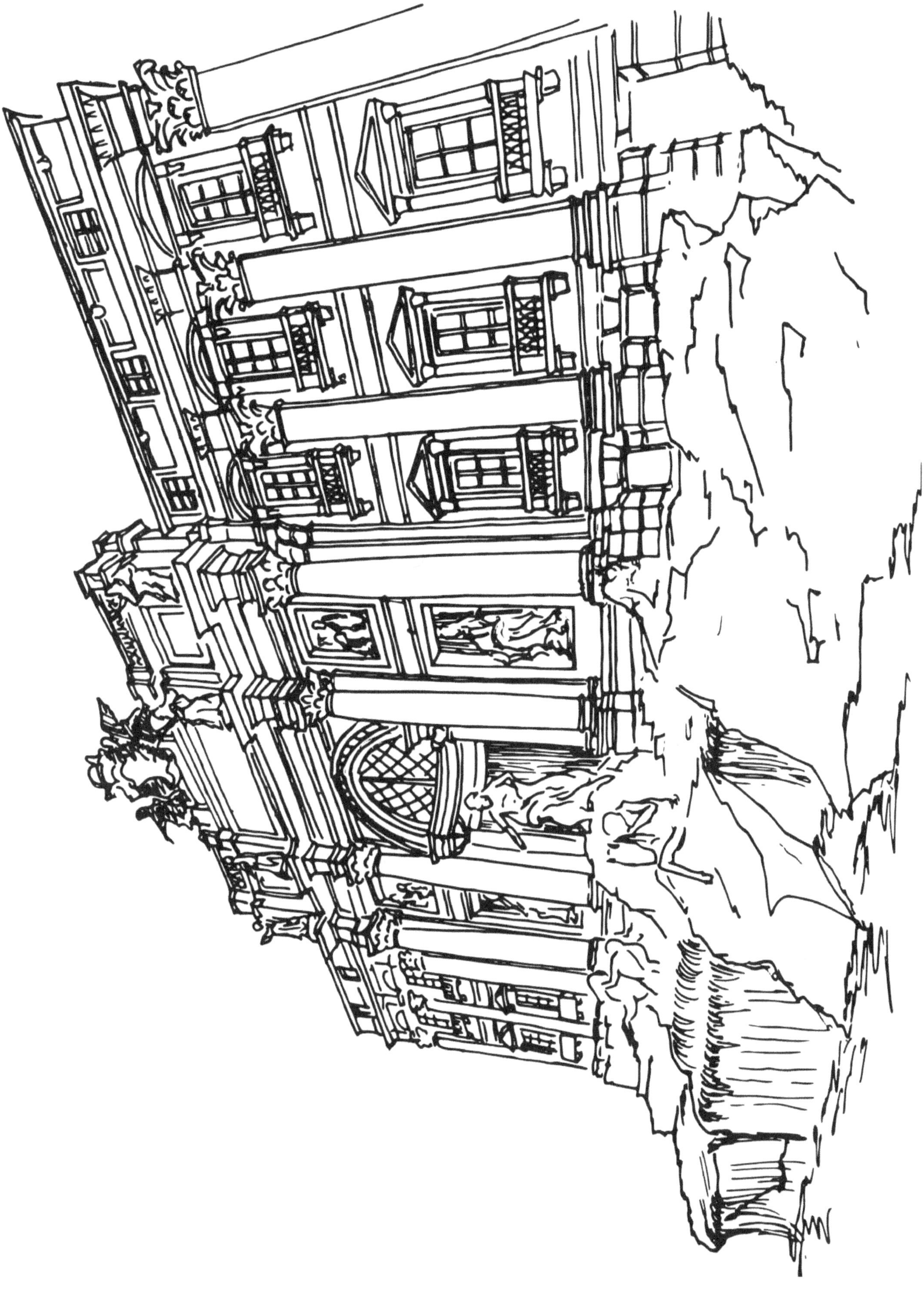

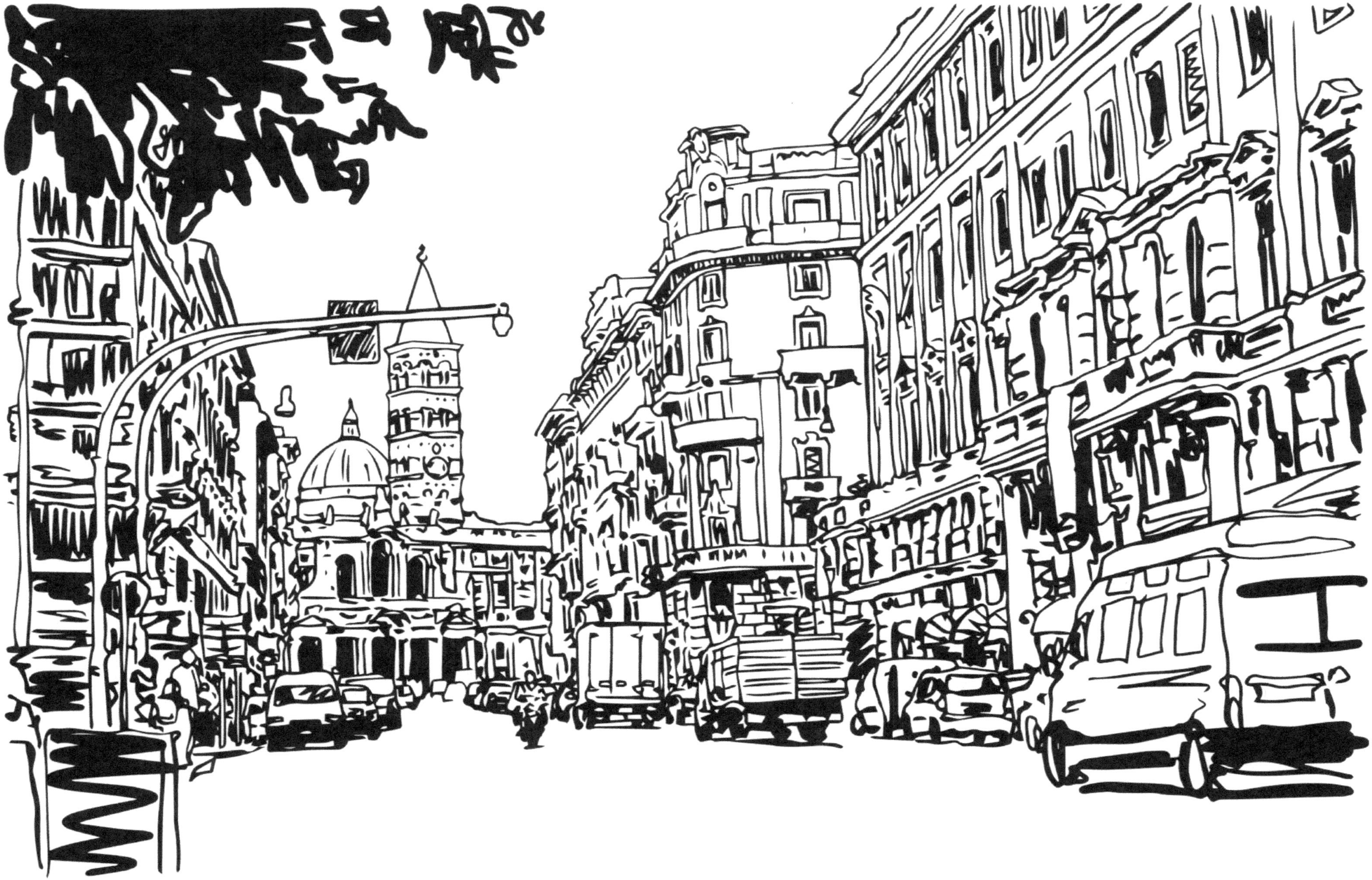

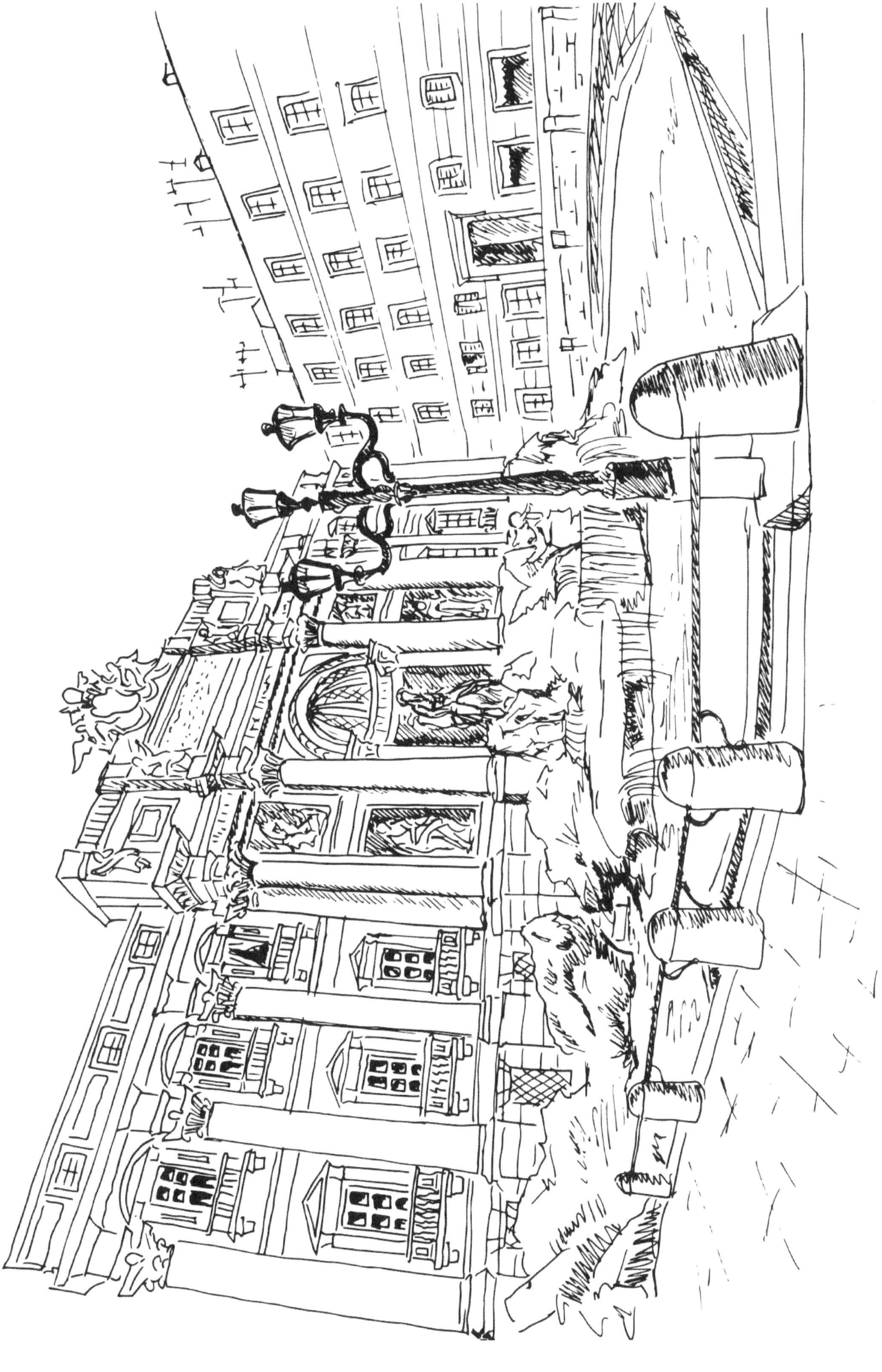

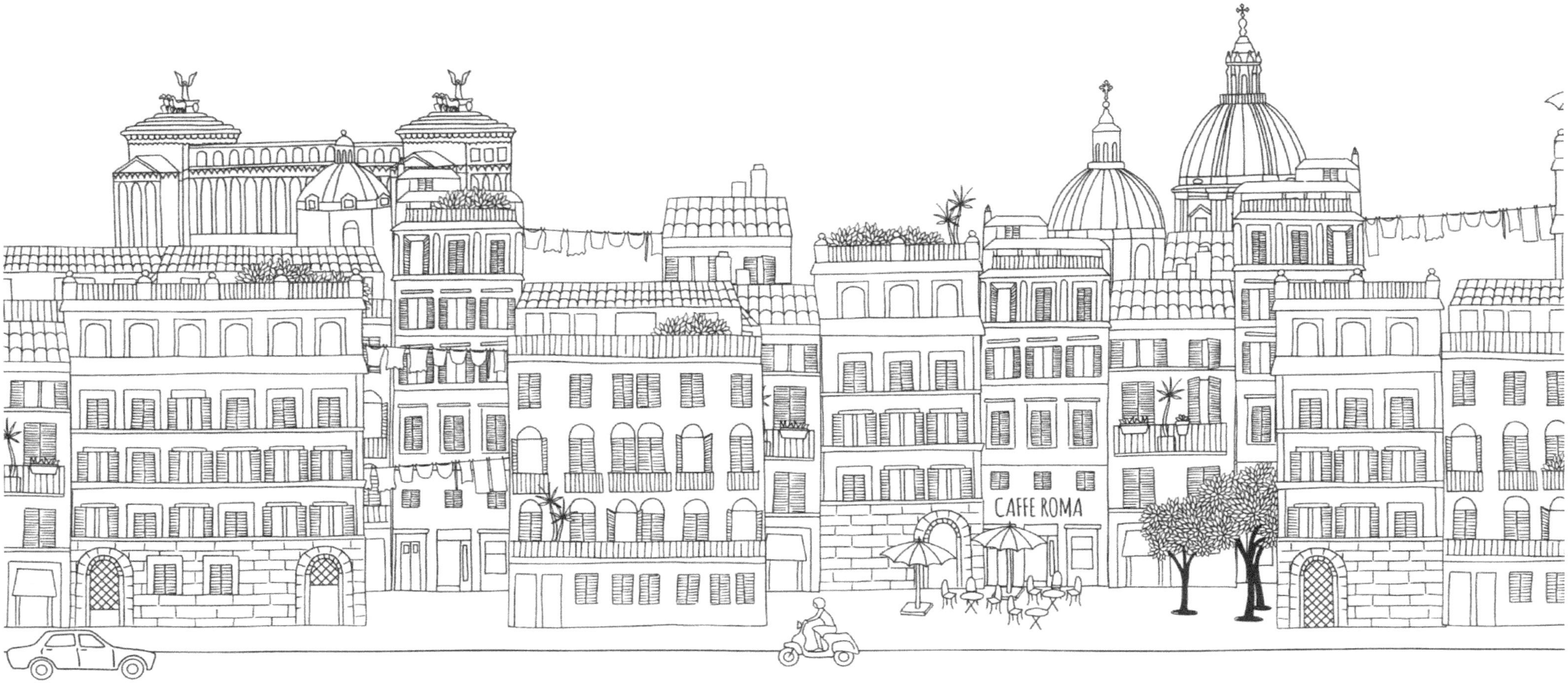
CAFFE ROMA

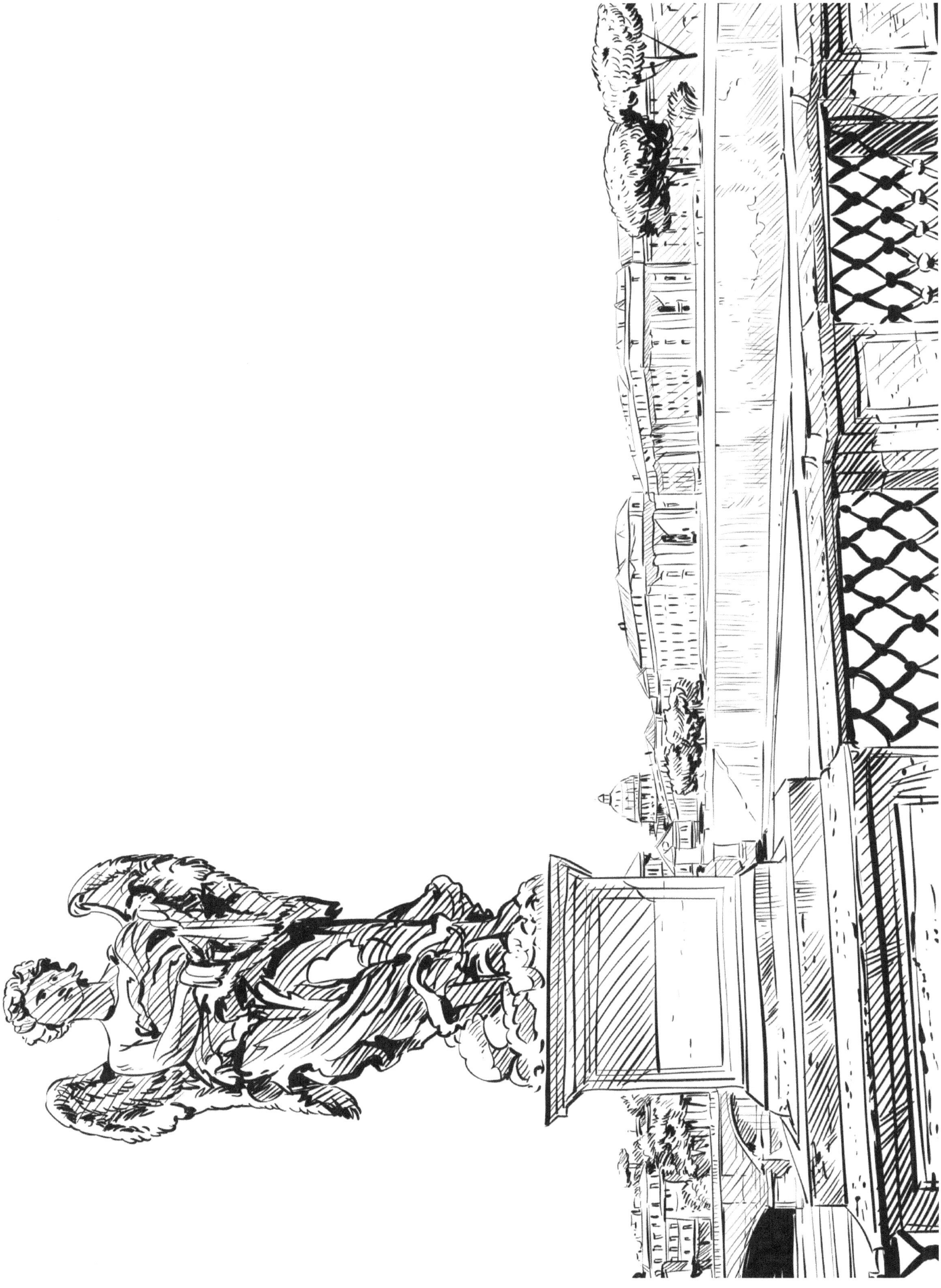

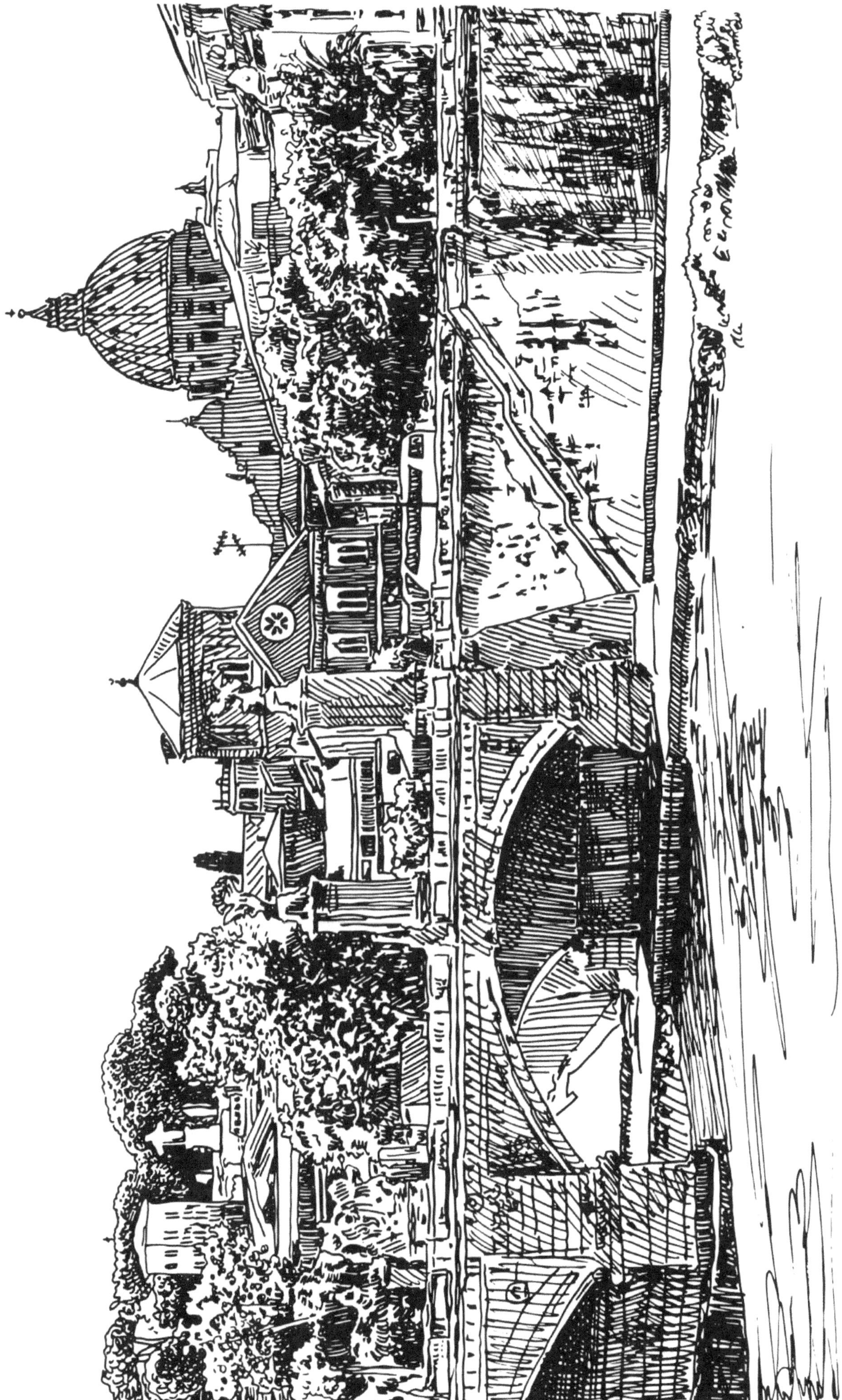

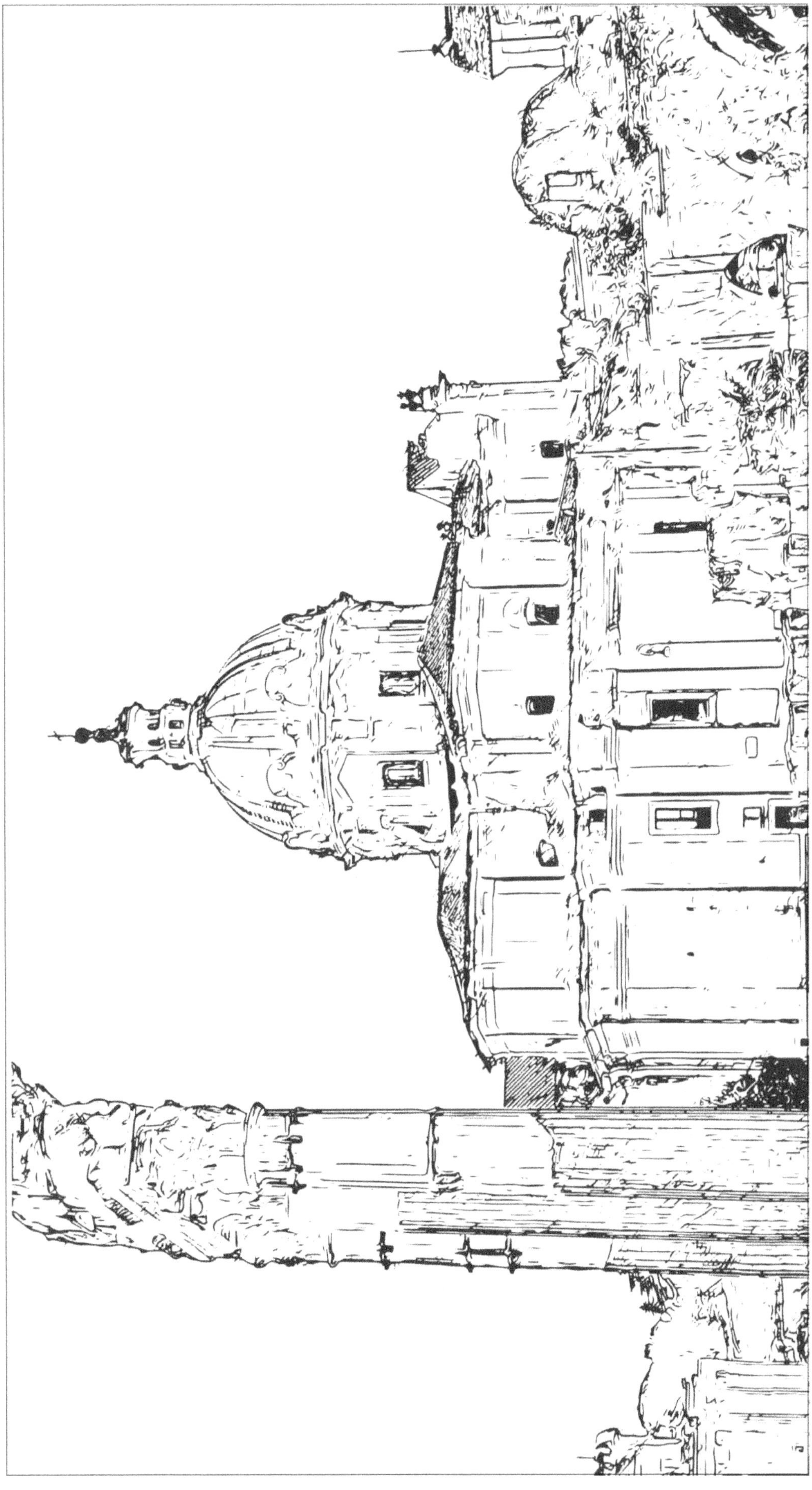

www.ingramcontent.com/pod-product-compliance
Lightning Source LLC
Chambersburg PA
CBHW080135240526
45468CB00009BA/2450
* 9 7 8 1 9 8 3 7 2 7 1 9 1 *